Mrs Brown's
SCRAPBOOK
ILLUSTRATED BY
Niki

For
Mr Brown
and Hannerl

COLLINS & BROWN

Shot by a dog

Tokyo, Jan 23.—A dog accidentally pulled the trigger of a shotgun with its legs, killing Yukiyasu Yazawa, the 12-year-old son of its owner, while all three were travelling in a car, police said.

Voyage by helmet

A police helmet lost when a constable was climbing from a ship off Colwyn Bay, Clwyd, last month, has been found on the Isle of Man, 70 miles away.

38 piranha victims

Rio de Janeiro, Nov. 15.—Man-eating piranha fish partially devoured 38 passengers when a bus carrying voters to polling stations for local elections plunged into a river in the Amazon jungle.

Pigeon post plan for blood tests

A plan to use pigeons to carry blood samples for urgent analysis has been devised by Mrs. Hilary Sanders, a work study officer with the South Weston Regional Health Authority at Plymouth.

A specimen of blood will be carried soon by a pathfinding pigeon on a test flight from Devonport Hospital, Plymouth, to the central haematology and pathology laboratories, two miles away.

A report by Mrs. Sanders, accepted in principle by the Plymouth health district, has considered the capital costs of 12 birds, a loft costing £220, and £50 a year for feed.

Part of a specimen needing urgent analysis would be attached to a pigeon and released. When it entered the laboratory loft it would break a photo-electric cell to alert technicians. Devonport staff would telephone to the laboratory to say that a specimen was in the air. If it should not arrive, or was damaged, another pigeon would be launched with the retained portion of the specimen.

Mrs. Sanders looked into the cost of using taxis for carrying specimens between hospitals and found that the district's bill was £25,000 last year, including £4,000 for Devonport Hospital. She predicts a saving of £1,000 a year for the hospital; the whole amount would not be saved because the birds would not fly in poor visibility.

A taxi takes 12 minutes to get to Devonport Hospital and another 10 minutes to get to the laboratory. A pigeon is expected to take less than five minutes.

Thumb bitten off by zebra restored

Sydney, Dec 8.—A circus trainer had his right thumb sown back on by surgeons today after a runaway zebra had bitten it off.

US woman carried foetus for 24 years

New York, May 12

A woman aged 75 who died in Montgomery, Alabama, last night was found to have a calcified foetus in her abdomen which she had apparently carried for about 24 years without knowing it. She was said to have been in good health in recent years.

The foetus was discovered while the woman was undergoing an operation for a gunshot wound received during a family quarrel a few hours before.

Members of her family said later that she had complained of a severe abdominal pain while lifting a heavy tub 24 years ago, but that the pain was diagnosed as being caused by a tumour and nothing more was done about it.

The foetus, which appeared to be nearly full-term, was the result of a rare abdominal pregnancy.

Woman buried in her Ferrari

New York, May 19.—Mrs Sandra West, the widow of an oil millionaire, was buried in San Antonio, Texas, today in a lace nightgown and sitting in her Ferrari car "with the seat slanted comfortably".

The request was made in her will and was granted by a California judge after being challenged in court.

Tango and the wolf

WOLVES love the tango; and at least one is captive in Leningrad Zoo because of his taste in music. The wolf had preyed on calves at a state farm near Minsk, and herdsmen at first scared him off with recorded howling of savage dogs. The wolf soon saw through that. But when he heard the distant strains of an old-fashioned tango played by a brass band, he stopped dead, sat on his haunches and bayed enthusiastically. So mesmerised was he that a herdsman could throw a coat over his head and pack him off to the zoo.

Sovetskaya Latviya, Riga

A slip of the driver's foot caused this car to burst through the wall of a multistorey car park and hang over a street in Tokyo.

Request in will for home to be demolished

Miss Marjorie Elvira Joan Lobb, who died in July, ordered in her will, published yesterday, that her home in Higher Town, Truro, Cornwall, be "levelled to the ground" and all furniture, personal belongings, plants and shrubs be destroyed "for sentimental reasons".

She left an estate worth £139,315 gross, £135,798 net.

Octogenarian wedding

Mr Edmond Cash, aged 89, a retired shepherd, and Mrs Mable Pyrah, aged 83, are to be married today in the parish church at Nettleham, Lincolnshire.

Tourists dogged

St Tropez — Two British tourists spent four days in jail here because white powder they bought to keep dogs away was thought by police to be heroin.

Second twin born safely

St Louis, Missouri — A woman, who miscarried one of her twin babies three and a half months ago, has successfully had the second twin, a 6lb 14oz baby.

Her doctor said the case was unique in the United States. Only one similar one existed – a German woman gave birth to a twin in 1978, 65 days after the first was delivered.

1,369 dogs on Chinese menu

Peking, Jan 3.—A restaurant in Jilin, north-east China, was praised by the *People's Daily* for capitalist-style enterprise in ensuring supplies of its most popular item—dog meat.

It appealed to people to bring in their own dogs to be eaten and it would buy them. The result: in under a month, it bought 1,369 dogs—a year's supply.

False trails

Elligras, South Africa.—A pair of fake rubber lion paws, used to lay false trails to attract big game hunters to the area, has been discovered here. The unnamed owner of a game ranch attracted hundreds of trophy hunters by walking around his farm wearing the lion paws.

The price of a good wife

Honiara, Solomon Islands – No matter how diligent, loving or attractive she may be, one cannot pay more than $600 (about £400) for a wife, the government of Temotu province in this former British Pacific colony has ruled. It passed legislation setting that as a maximum price for a bride.

Anyone paying more faces a hearing before the Council of Chiefs and three months in jail, or a fine of up to £60. Wife-buying is a common practice here.

Fish falsely described

Alan Burness, a pet shop owner, of Market Street, Shrewsbury, was fined £40 yesterday for selling a "breeding pair" of goldfish that turned out to be two females.

Struck down

Andy Thompson, 24, was seriously ill in an intensive care unit last night after being struck by lightning playing football at Lydney, Gloucestershire. All 22 players, the linesmen and referee were knocked to the the ground. Three players were taken to hospital. Two were released after being treated for shock.

Fatal pass

Peking — Vilong, an amorous female elephant aged 42, and Baibao, her 53-year-old mate, died in Canton Zoo after he rebuffed her advances and they landed on top of each other in a narrow moat. Baibao died of shock and Vilong injured her lungs struggling out and died later.

Woman shoots driver

Los Angeles, Dec 29.—A woman aged 70 shot dead a young man who refused to move the car he had parked in front of her drive. Police failed to find the woman, who, witnesses said, walked off after the shooting.

Now sheep may safely graze

A visit to the dentist's chair has made grazing more pleasurable for 60 ewes on a Ministry of Agriculture farm at Preston Wynne, Hereford and Worcester.

They have been fitted with false teeth, a development which could save farmers thousands of pounds because, until now, sheep with bad teeth had to be culled as they could not eat. Mr David Brown, in charge of the project, said the sheep sat in a padded chair, similar to those used by dentists.

Italy baffled by breathing from tomb of baroness

Rome, Sept 10

The 230 inhabitants of the village of Bombardone near Pavia had been used to a quiet life (despite the name of the place) until the breathing of a dead baroness began on a summer's night in mid-August.

The first to hear it was a young man who was walking his girlfriend near the villaget cemetery and heard the sound of breathing from within the chapel which contains the bones of the baroness and her husband.

She was a dancer from Rome of humble origins who married Baron Giuseppe Weilweiss. He died in 1939 " almost " as local reports have it " mad ". His wife, Giselda, lived a totally secluded life for 20 years until she too died at 82, and was placed in a sarcophagus alongside her husband.

It was said that breathing from her tomb can be heard every night until sunrise.

The chapel and the cellar beneath were searched for snakes or other creatures that might make a noise similar to a woman's breathing and a pair of owls were discovered in the vaulted ceiling.

The mystery appeared solved. The digestive processes of a large owl could, it was thought, be mistaken for the breathing of a woman who would now, if still alive, be aged 103. A new home was found for the owls and the opening through which they entered was closed.

But the breathing continued.

Killer shower

Harare   – A municipal worker sent to cut off power at a house in Gweru clipped the wrong wire, making the water pipes live. The occupant, defaulting on payments took a shower and was killed.

Bride aged 93

Mary Roach, aged 93, and David Powell, aged 84, were married at St Peter's Church, Pontardawe, near Swansea, yesterday. They live in an old people's home in the town.

Astrofrog

Jakarta   – Indonesia is to put a giant Sumatran frog, 30in long, on board the US space shuttle in June, together with a woman scientist, aged 33, and an Indonesian satellite.

Cyclists advised not to use narrow saddles

Cyclists may become sexually impotent from pressure on nerves by the bicycle saddle, an American doctor says in the *New England Journal of Medicine*, the leading United States weekly journal for doctors.

Dr John D. Goodson, of the Massachusetts General Hospital in Boston, describes a man who lost sensation in his penis after a 180-mile bicycle ride and became impotent.

The cause was found to be damage to the pudendal nerves from his narrow, hard leather bicycle seat. He was advised to use a wider seat and his symptoms resolved within a month.

Compression of the pudendal nerves is a hazard of cycling that may affect the sexual response in both men and women, Dr Goodson says. Either the seat should be padded or it should be sloped downwards to relieve the risk of damaging pressure.

Birthday party

The birth of twins to Mrs Susan Dwyer, of Oxford, on her birthday on Tuesday has produced a family of four all with the same birthday. Her husband was also born on the same date.

Mummified baby's body 40 years old

The mummified body of a baby born more than 40 years ago was found in a suitcase when the sisters of a spinster were sorting out her possessions after her death. Dr Rufus Crompton, a pathologist, told a Battersea inquest yesterday that the baby was either stillborn or survived only two or three days.

He said he could not ascertain its sex or the cause of death and added that the baby had been born between 40 and 70 years ago.

Growing pain

Mr Ken Wood of Tavistock, Devon, is to sell his £11,500 custom-built Morgan sports car, after waiting seven years for delivery, because he has gained two stone in weight and cannot get into the car.

Killer cable

Chester, Texas   – A steel cable snapped at a sawmill, decapitating the owner and three employees. A fifth man was injured.

Pieces of ex-lover's body kept in freezer

Mönchengladbach, West Germany   – A 26-year-old woman has admitted strangling her lover, sawing up his corpse, cooking parts of it and storing the pieces in her home freezer for almost a year.

Police said 10 video films with brutal cannibalism scenes were siezed.

Flea traps set

Flea traps have been set in the Welsh Office building in Cardiff after civil servants complained they were being bitten.

Oldest marriage ends

The longest marriage in Britain has ended with the death on Tuesday of Mrs Harriet Orton, of Great Gidding, near Peterborough, aged 103.

She and her husband, Mr John Orton, aged 105, would have celebrated their eighty-first wedding anniversary in July.

Retribution

Peking   – A woman who nailed her invalid father-in-law into a coffin and had him buried alive has been executed.

Age concern

Mrs Eva Alcock, of Kingswinford, West Midlands, the widow of a vicar, left orders in her will for her age not to be made known and her date of birth not to put on her tombstone or coffin. She died last September.

Church change for TV

Evensong at St Luke's Lowick, Cumbria, near Coniston Water, has been brought forward by 45 minutes after an appeal to the rural dean by parishioners who want to make sure of seeing the BBC television series *All creatures Great and Small*.

NOSE BITER JAILED

A court in Knopstrup, Denmark, sentenced a 28-year-old man to 18 months in prison for biting off the end of his wife's nose during a domestic squabble. Her face was restored after plastic surgery.

TEA GETS THE BIRD

Two cockatoos that constantly shrieked " Alma, I want a cup of tea " were put to flight by a Sydney court yesterday. Alma and William Rash were ordered to move their birds from a block of flats where they disturbed residents.

MARITAL CLASH

Richard Schwabe, driving a Cortina, was in collision with his wife, Lyn, driving a Viva, near a junction close to their home in Glanville Road, Hadley, Su:olk. Mrs Schwabe was released after hospital treatment; her husband was unhurt.

Piano used in suicide`

Paris, April 2.—A young man committed suicide by causing a piano to crush his skull as he lay on a bed, police said today.

The man, from Vincennes, outside Paris, pulled a cord to tip over the piano, which had been balanced precariously across a plank above his bed.

SLAKING THAT TIGER'S THIRST

The Indan Government is planning to build troughs of fresh water in the mangrove swamps of Bengal to stop attacks by tigers.

Man-eating tigers kill about 40 people a year in the Sunderbans region because they lack fresh water. according to research by the World Wildlife Fund. Living on salt water causes a chemical imbalance which they correct by eating human beings.

' Vampire ' executed

Warsaw, May 3.—Zdislaw Marchwicki, an ex-miner, aged 50, known as the Vampire of Katowice, who once confessed to killing " perhaps 20 or 26 women ". has been executed for murder.

Dolphins save sea lion

Moscow, Aug 15.—A sea lion surrounded by killer whales cried out for help and was saved by dolphins who formed a ring round it, Tass said. The rescue was seen by Soviet fishermen off Kamchatka.

Baby born with four legs

Doctors are preparing to carry out a rare and delicate operation on a six-weeks-old baby boy with four legs. He was born in a hospital in Lincolnshire and moved to Sheffield Children's Hospital.

The hospital said : " The purpose of the operation will be to remove as much of the handicap as possible, and the surgeon is hopeful of a high degree of success."

Extra legs removed

A boy aged three months from Lincolnshire, who was born with four legs, had two legs and a pelvic bone removed at Sheffield Children's Hospital yesterday. He was said to be doing well.

HOOLIGAN ROOM

A £1 million leisure centre to be built at Grantham, Lincs, is to include a room for hooligans to carry out their rowdy activities.

Couple glued together

A prisoner and his wife were taken to hospital from a courtroom in Whitminster, Gloucestershire, yesterday, after bonding themselves together with superglue.

Edward Szuluk, aged 27, had been remanded in custody for a week on an assault charge when his wife Wendy, aged 25, entered a detention room with the glue on her palms. They locked hands and police could not tear them apart.

The couple, from Southway, Plymouth, were taken to the Gloucestershire Royal Hospital Gloucester, where doctors prised them apart.

GUARD DOG STOLEN

A guard dog, Sammy, eight-year-old St Bernard, was the only thing stolen when thieves raided a timber yard at Havant, Hants, police said yesterday.

The driver of an empty bus escaped with minor injuries when it skidded and came to rest on a motorway parapet near Chicago.

Elephant dies chewing electric cable

Stockholm, Dec 20.—A circus elephant waiting to perform in a show near here died when it seized a high voltage power cable with its trunk and chewed it.

Larger than life

Sydney — Hunted by 20 police, a helicopter, a man with a tranquillizer gun, and television crew, a lion or cougar reported prowling through a Sydney suburb turned out to be Ginger, a factory tomcat.

Man in sleeping bag is run over by friend

Mr Anthony Day, aged 47, a parachute instructor, was recovering in hospital last night after being accidently run over by his friend as he slept in a sleeping bag in the driveway.

Mr Day had returned to the house in Fair Oak, Hampshire, early yesterday morning after spending six months on a camping expedition in Israel. He was locked out of the lodgings and so decided to wait until his friend Mr Joseph Lambert, arrived home from his night-shift work.

Mr Day settled down to sleep on the driveway in front of the garage door. The next thing he knew was when the MG sportscar ran over him, pinning him to the ground.

Mr Lambert, a welder, aged 54, said: "I was horrified. I had just come home from the Fawley refinery, turned into the steep driveway, and saw a bag on the ground.

"I though it was an empty kit bag and drove over it to get to the garage. It wasn't until I opened the garage doors that I saw Tony's legs wiggling in the bag.

"I ran for the fire brigade and police and then dashed back to help my friend. Fortunately I had an old air bag and was able to jack the car up."

The Royal Hampshire County Hospital in Winchester said last night that Mr Day had several broken ribs and blurred vision.

Husband saws his home in half

VIRGIL EVERHART, 57, who is being sued for divorce by his estranged wife, decided to begin the property settlement on his own — cutting their house in half with a chain saw.

By the time he stopped today for a rest he had cut through most of the flooring in the two-storey house in Central City, Kentucky.

"I need to get a cutting torch to divide the bathtub," he added.

Janice Everhart, 36, who moved out of the house two weeks ago with their two children, could not be reached for comment. Asked what his wife's reaction might be, Everhart said: "She might have a heart attack."

He said that he plans to live in his half of the house.

Wormburgers recommended by health experts

Hongkong, Nov 20.

Cooked worms and insects are being recommended on Chinese menus in Hongkong, Manila, Tokyo and South-east Asian capitals since a recent, widely publicized health report by Philippine experts on the nutrition potential of edible termites.

Boiled or fried worms and insects, usually mixed with eggs or rice, are regularly eaten in China and are occasionally requested by expatriate gourmets in Chinese restaurants abroad. The dish is generally called *Wo-chung*.

It is pointed out that the worms and termites need not be restricted to Chinese-style cooking but can be served agreeably as wormburgers and worm omelettes, Western-style.

Some Japanese *sumo* wrestlers devour the worms raw by the cupful.

According to the experts, edible termites offer 11 different nutrients—chiefly carbohydrates and proteins.

The thief who came to dinner

MOSCOW, Wednesday

A BURGLAR who took a leisurely bath and had a snack in his victim's flat was caught when he could not resist an urge to play the piano.

A bit dim

Moscow. — A Soviet factory which made 13,000 pairs of sunglasses so dark that even the sun was obscured to their wearers and produced more than 3,000 plastic footballs that burst when they were kicked, has been named by Tass as an example of the indifferent management plaguing Soviet industry.

Two-tongued

Miami — A two-headed water snake has become reigning reptile at the Miami serpentarium, munching six goldfish at a time with both heads.

Monk jailed

Seoul — A 34-year-old South Korean Buddhist monk has been sentenced to life imprisonment for killing a fellow monk in a fight over the control of a temple last August.

Dry season

Lusaka — Zambia's two main bottling plants are at a standstill because they have no bottle tops.

Cannibal fear

Kampala — Ugandan police have arrested 11 people on suspicion of cannibalism after they were found cooking what was believed to be human flesh in pots.

Drug helped prayers, nun claims

Athens, Aug 21.—A nun was in jail in the northern Greek town of Patras today after her superior at the Pepolinitsis convent there found her smoking cannabis in her cell.

Sister Flothee, aged 48, is alleged to have grown the drug in the convent garden. She is said to have told police at Patras that she smoked cannabis as it helped her to "participate" more in her prayers.

She denied planting the drug and maintained that it was "God's breezes" which blew seeds into the convent. She is to appear in court.

Foxes return

Thirty foxes who were released from a breeding farm at Kingham, Oxfordshire, by an animal rights group returned to the farm through a hole which the protesters had cut in a fence.

Blood and sex attacks by 'vampire'

A 22-YEAR-OLD student has been arrested as a "modern-day vampire" for drinking the blood of girls he drugged and seduced, police in Frankfurt said yesterday.

The student, whose name was not released, was taken into custody after the mother of a 15-year-old girl reported the alleged assaults.

The woman said her daughter claimed the student had seduced a number of 12 to 15-year-olds with the help of drugs and drawn off quantities of their blood for drinking.

Butcher's knives

A search of the student's home turned up syringes and bottles with traces of human blood, drugs and chemicals and four large butcher knives.

Police said the student initially denied his involvement, but later said he had drawn off blood from friends because he was interested in making blood tests.

A 14-year-old youth told police that the student had recently emptied a bucket of blood from the apartment because it was rotting.

An arrest warrant said the student is under "urgent suspicion" of causing dangerous bodily injuries, seducing minors and possesing illegal drugs.

£300 IN NOTES GO DOWN THE DRAIN

Police in County Durham are looking for someone who is literally pouring money down the drain.

Workmen at a sewage works at Tanfield Lea, near Stanley, found torn up money, including £5 notes and £10 notes, in the main sewer this week. So far more than £300 has been recovered. An official said the cash could not have been in the system more than 24 hours.

A police spokesman said: "We are anxious to trace where the money is coming from. It could be a child who has got hold of his father's pay packet or savings, or it could be an old person."

Going steady

John Orton, 102, and his wife Harriet, 100, today celebrate their 78th wedding anniversary. They will have a family party at the village of Great Gidding, near Huntingdon, where they have lived for 75 years.

Villagers fight snake

Dacca, July 3.—Villagers in north-west Bangladesh fought a tug-of-war with a 30ft python which swallowed a man up to the waist, but both died in the struggle.

LEG COVER-UP

Yesterday's issue of the Kuwaiti newspaper AL-WATAN was banned by the government for publishing a picture of a woman's leg. The government order said the picture offended public morality.

Dog's season ticket

The Hague, June 20.—Dogs travelling regularly on buses and trams in The Hague won the right today to hold a young person's season ticket if they carry an identity card with their photograph, name and owner's name.

Marriage lasted as long as the reception

Married life for Teresa Wignall, aged 16, lasted only as long as the wedding reception, it was stated in the Family Division of the High Court yesterday.

After the guests left, her bridegroom, Eric, aged 21, also left, to go to work on a night shift as an hotel chef. He never returned to live with her.

The judge granted Mrs Wignall, now aged 20, of Hazelwood Crescent, North Kensington, London, a decree nisi of nullity because of the refusal of her husband, now aged 25, to consummate their marriage.

After yesterday's undefended hearing, which Mr Wignall did not attend, Mrs Wignall said: "We had known each other for two years, since I was 14."

JAIL BREAK-IN

Thieves broke into Channings Wood prison, near Newton Abbot, Devon, yesterday, and stole a ton of copper tubing valued at £1,000.

'GRANDMA' CHIMP MOTHER AT 32

Meg, a 32-year-old chimpanzee at Chester Zoo has surprised experts by becoming a mother long after the normal lifespan of her species. She has given birth to a 3lb 6oz baby, Gemma, her 15th baby in 23 years.

"The human equivalent would be a woman of 60 to 65 having a baby," a zoo official said. "We believe that Meg must surely be a candidate for the "Guinness Book of Records." Baby Gemma rejected by her mother, is now being hand-reared by the zoo's curator and his wife.

Snail-eater dies

Nancy, France, Nov 26.—M Marc Quinquandon, the world snail-eating champion, died of indigestion in hospital yesterday after eating 72 snails in three minutes.

ONE TOO MANY

Plans to open a public house opposite a hostel for alcoholics in Northampton have been dropped. Area Health officials said the pub would be too much of a temptation.

Crocodile hunt

Darwin, Sept 19.—Hunters are searching for an 18ft crocodile said to have attacked and sunk two fishing boats, devouring the petrol tank of one of them.

Empire State jump : Elvita Adams, aged 29, recovering in a New York hospital yesterday after jumping from the observation platform on the eighty-sixth floor of the Empire State building and suffering only a broken leg. Police said she was caught by a strong gust of wind and was blown on to a ledge on the storey below. A security officer opened a window and pulled the moaning woman to safety.

Grisly find

TWO bears, skinned and headless, were found floating in London's River Lea last night. Police have no idea how they got there. A Scotland Yard spokesman said: "Your guess is as good as mine. They're not a particularly common species in the Lea Valley."

Miracle baby

Roanoke, Virginia — An 11oz girl was born yesterday to a clinically dead woman who had been kept breathing mechanically for 84 days since suffering a seizure in April.

Grave issue

Villagers of Laneham, Nottinghamshire, have threatened to boycott the institution as vicar on Friday of the Rev Geoffrey Holliday because he put sheep to graze in the curchyards to cut costs. The villages say the sheep are eating flowers on the graves.

Saved by bell

Satellite Beach, Florida — A telephone bell saved Mr Hilton Mortin. whose lavatory blew up after he had cleaed it with two differnt detergents. "It sounded like a hand granade," he said.

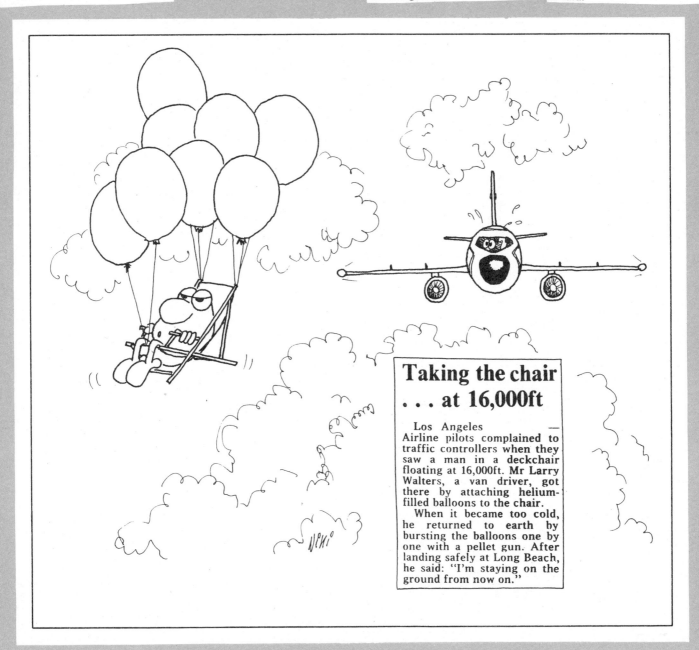

Taking the chair ... at 16,000ft

Los Angeles — Airline pilots complained to traffic controllers when they saw a man in a deckchair floating at 16,000ft. Mr Larry Walters, a van driver, got there by attaching helium-filled balloons to the chair.

When it became too cold, he returned to earth by bursting the balloons one by one with a pellet gun. After landing safely at Long Beach, he said: "I'm staying on the ground from now on."

Move to ban mouse racing

The Royal Society for the Prevention of Cruelty to Animals may take legal action to end a wave of mouse racing meetings in public houses and clubs.

A recent meeting at the Three Tuns Hotel at Honiton in Devon, attended by 65 enthusiasts, is being investigated by the society, which says mouse races are cruel and illegal. The organizer of the Honiton event has denied any cruelty.

Fainting gunman

Swansea, Massachusetts — A bungling bank robber fainted when the woman cashier he held up at gunpoint said she had no money. He had also locked his getaway car with the keys inside.

Record sneeze

Tricia Reay, aged 12, of Springfield Road, Sutton Coldfield, has scored a world record for Britain by sneezing non-stop for 156 days.

Bully for Bison and red cow

Moscow — A European bison and a Lithuanian red cow have spawned an unusually large but nimble long-haired heifer which could revolutionize cattle breeding, Tass reported yesterday.

"The heifer grew like baker's dough and put on 4lb within 24 hours -- twice as much as normal cattle offspring. Now the animal weighs half a tonne," Tass said.

Unlucky gambol

Mrs Ivy Scott, aged 67, of Kineton, Warwickshire, suffered a broken arm and back injuries when butted and knocked down by a neighbour's pet lamb called Herbie.

Death-wish Daniel dies in lion's den

A SPANIARD, Jesus de la Mora, finally succeeded yesterday in his bizarre death wish to be killed and eaten by lions.

It was his third attempt in 10 days to clamber over the high wire safety netting that separates visitors from the 40 lions at a safari park at Vendrell, near the resort town of Sitges, on Spain's east coast.

Twice guards hauled him back to safety and finally handed him over to the Civil Guards. For the third time Mora, a 31-year-old bachelor, from Barcelona, returned to the park and managed to get to the fence unnoticed.

Once over the fence, Mora ran shouting and waving his arms towards a group of the animals, which attacked and killed him. By the time the lions were driven off, the body had been half eaten.

Freed by police

Francisco Angulo, director of the park, which attracted three million visitors last year, most of them foreign holidaymakers, said yesterday: "Twice before we managed to stop him. We handed him over to the police. But they released him for lack of charges.

"He returned in the early morning for a third time and we could not keep the lions from getting him."

It was the second time in four years that the lions have killed a man at the park. The first victim was a Frenchman on his honeymoon who disobeyed warnings and got out of his car to take photographs.

Diet man wanted stomach surgery to be reversed

A 20-stone man who had failed to diet adequately, despite having his teeth wired together for nine months, underwent an operation to reduce the size of his stomach.

But he asked for the operation to be reversed when he found he was unable to eat satisfactorily, an inquest at Hornsey, north London, was told yesterday. His health began to fail, the wound refused to heal because of malnutrition, and after four more operations he died.

Dive for a finger

Adelaide, Dec 19.—An 11-year-old boy dived into a public swimming pool to retrieve the little finger of his right hand, severed moments earlier on a water slide. Surgeons sewed it on again.

Personal delivery

Toulouse, Feb 1.—A 77-year-old man entered a hospital here today, told the caretaker that he was donating his body to science and shot himself dead through the head. His body was accepted.

7oz baby lives

Jakarta, Feb 22.—A "miniature" premature baby girl, weighing only 7oz at birth in Java three weeks ago, was today reported to be doing well after doctors predicted that she would live only a few days. She now weighs 21oz.

Dog shoots passer-by with master's rifle

Luneville, France, Nov 8.—A man walking in the street here was shot in the shoulder by a dog firing from an hotel window, police said today. The dog had playfully grabbed his master's hunting rifle when he put it down by the window and it went off accidentally.

'MIRACULOUS' MOVEMENT WAS A RAID

The mantle on the statue of a Madonna began moving slightly and the stunned faithful gathered at a parish church in southern Italy thought a miracle was under way.

"Miracolo, Miracolo," some shouted, and women fainted.

But the cause of movement was in fact more prosaic — a thief was stealing jewels knitted to the mantle behind the altar in Pietrelcina. He got away with gems, gifts of the faithful valued at more than £12,000.

Twins—one black and one white

A WOMAN who had sex with a white man and a black man on the same day give birth nine months later to twin boys, one white and one black, according to testimony at a paternity hearing made public in West Germany yesterday. Scientists said she could have ovulated twice on the day in question.

Both men—a white German and a black American soldier—denied paternity. The woman sued the German on behalf of the white twin, but lost because of evidence that she had several sexual partners around the relevant time. The twins have been placed with separate foster parents and the mother has since married another man.

Death comes at 143

Moscow, Nov 14.—Mr Medzhid Agayev, one of the oldest inhabitants of the Soviet Union, has died at the age of 143 in the highland village of Tikyaband, Azerzaijan.

HUNTING 'KILLS'

Two people died and two were critically injured during the first 24 hours of Italy's annual hunting season, according to police.

The 6ft tall female bear which escaped from Dudley Zoo yesterday was finally captured on a zebra crossing where she was cornered by three police panda cars.

Japan gets a shot of instant whisky

Tokyo, Feb 4

After the success of instant coffee, barmen of the future might soon toss a teaspoon of powder into a glass of ice and water to produce scotch on the rocks, a martini or an after-dinner brandy.

Mrs Brown hopes for a storybook ending

007 for Russia

Berne, June 23.—Swiss telephone subscribers, who will be able to dial direct to the Soviet Union from July 1, should have no trouble remembering the code, which is 007. Any connexion with James Bond, the fictional spy, is said to be unintentional.

A day's food for Gunvor Rosén of Kalmar, Sweden, who has to eat 20,000 calories a day because she has Crohn's disease and has undergone abdominal surgery. She lives next to a hospital where she eats 11 meals a day.

Zeng Jinlian, of Yujiang village in central China, who is believed to have become the world first eight-foot giantess, so dethroning England's Ginny Bunford (1895-1922), whose skeleton is preserved in Birmingham.

Talking parrot alerts police

Chico, California, Sept 30.—A young man was arrested after a stolen parrot he brought into a pet shop started reciting its name. The bird's owner had alerted shop owners should anyone try to sell it. A salesman called police after the parrot started telling everyone who he was.

STRIP SHOW STUDENTS EXPELLED

Johannesburg, Nov 11

Sixteen students have been expelled from South Africa's leading university for theological studies for attending a strip show. They were brought before a disciplinary committee at the Potchefstroom University for Christian Higher Education in the south-west Transvaal after a party to celebrate the end of the academic year.

They had hired a stripper to entertain them in factory premises well away from the university.

The complete spy kit

Wellington. A briefcase lost by a New Zealand intelligence agent has been found with its contents intact. They included secret documents, three meat pies, two slices of cake and a sex magazine, intelligence sources said.

Mr Paul Molineaux, the security service director, said he had ordered a full inquiry. But he said that he did not think New Zealand's security had been compromised by the discovery, made by a 10-year-old boy.

FULL NAVAL BURIAL FOR SHIP'S CAT

Rochester

Able seaman Charlie the cat was buried yesterday with full naval honours.

The bugler played the Last Post, the flag was lowered to half mast and the officer of the watch read the service at the HMS Pembroke offices at Chatham Naval Base, Kent, where Charlie was officially listed as a member of staff.

Chief Petty Officer Roger Leeder said: "He was our ship's cat and as such a full member of the crew."

Charlie, who was run over on Sunday, had his own security pass and was entered in the wage book as receiving board and food.

300 at family reunion

Nearly 300 people with the surname of Loxton drank a toast to one another in the village of Loxton, near Weston-super-Mare, Avon, yesterday at a reunion. They had come from Australia, Canada, America and South Africa, as well as from many parts of Britain.

Scientists hope to create live mammoth

Moscow, Jan 21

A living mammoth, identical to those that roamed the world thousands of years ago, may be recreated from the single cell of a frozen carcase found recently in Siberia, if Soviet experiments are successful.

A member of the Soviet Academy of Sciences recently told a newspaper that living cells from the almost perfectly preserved body of a mammoth that died 44,000 years ago could theoretically be reproduced in a laboratory and cultured to produce a living creature.

Dr V. Mikhelson, a research scientist at the Institute of Cytology, said the process had already been successfully tested with frogs.

Two years ago a baby mammoth nicknamed Dima—since displayed at an exhibition in London last year—was found in a frozen marsh in Siberia, and Soviet scientists discovered cells that were in almost perfect condition in its kidney and liver.

Dr Mikhelson said: "As soon as we get a living cell out of any part of the mammoth body we shall fuse it together in a test tube with the sex cell of a female Indian elephant whose nucleus will first be irradiated by X-ray.

"This cell will then be implanted in the organism of the female elephant. And under favourable conditions after 18 to 20 months, the normal pregnancy period, the world's first 'artificial' mammoth will be born."

Dr Mikhelson said that further investigations jointly with American scientists at Wain State University in Michigan had found well preserved blood cells in Dima's body.

By the time Dr Mikhelson arrived in Magadan, in the Soviet Far East, most of Dima's organs had already been put in formalin. But he was lucky to get hold of some still-frozen tissue which was taken to Leningrad and preserved in a laboratory.

The first attempts to culture living cells from this tissue failed, but the scientists then tried the tissues from another mammoth found in 1978.

At one point it seemed as though a culture had begun to grow in the test tube. But, Dr Mikhelson said, a mistake was made and the experiment ruined.

He has now begun with a third female mammoth found at a different location. Henceforth every group of scientists investigating newly-discovered mammoths in the permafrost will include a cytologist. "We have to get the tissues before they are unfrozen," he explained. "Sooner or later we shall succeed."

A fellow academician told the newspaper *Trud* that the principles of biology, genetics and cytology (study of cells) did not rule out the possibility of such experiments. The problem was to get laboratory conditions right for the culture of the cells.

Cloning, the reproduction of cells from a single living cell, has long been known to scientists in the West.

But western experts in Moscow said experiments in this field had so far been limited to simpler organisms such as bacteria and unicellular structures, and it was doubtful whether such an ambitious project as recreating an extinct mammoth was yet possible.

SANTAS IN PITCH BATTLE

The seasonal spirit did not stretch very far when two Father Christmases spotted each other in a crowded street. Both were heading for the same pitch to sell their wares.

Clerkenwell Court, in London, heard yesterday how tempers became frayed and voices raised as Santas, David Cooper and William Woolf, challenged each other for the right to use the pitch, in Kingsway.

Mothers and children watched in amazement as they came to blows. "The fur was really flying", Police Constable Derek Spencer, who arrested them said.

Heart surgeon stole violins

Curse fails to impress judge

San Francisco. — A judge has ruled that a police lieutenant was not struck down by Osiris, the Egyptian god of the dead, while guarding treasures from the tomb of Tutankhamun.

Lieutentant George La Brash, aged 56, suffered a stroke during the Tutankhamun exhibition in 1979. He sued unsuccessfully for £9,700 lost in wages while recovering.

BITTER FROGS

Peking, June 5.—In a rare battle, more than 2,000 frogs bit and tore at each other for two hours in a rice field in south China's Hunan province. A child threw a rock, and they fled, leaving 43 dead. According to an evening paper, several dozen frogs started fighting after heavy rain in April. The urgent croaking of the combatants brought reinforcements.—

Baby buried

Dhaka — A newborn boy was found alive in the northern Tangail district 24 hours after being buried to save his unmarried teenaged mother from the penalties for illegal sex, Bangladesh police said yesterday.

Papa pays fine for reluctant fiddler

Corporation bus crews in Nottingham could not understand why the same violin was left on buses once a fortnight for two months and had to be claimed at the lost-property office. An official explained yesterday that it belonged to a little girl who did not want to go to music lessons.

After paying the lost-property charge for the fourth time her father said: "She will learn the violin even if it kills me."

TOOTH REMOVED FROM EAR

A tooth carefully wrapped in tissue paper has been syringed from the ear of Mrs Janet Bibby, 35, of Keats Way, Higham Ferrers, Northants after she complained to her docor of deafness. She believes it became lodged in her ear nearly 30 years ago.

"I must have put it on my pillow hoping the fairies would bring me sixpence" she said. "It obviously became lodged in my ear after I had fallen asleep."

Actress killed by press cuttings

New York, Dec 20.—Miss Eleanor Barry, aged 70, a former actress, died after a pile of press cuttings, newspapers and books fell on her at home.

Police said today that the house she shared with her sister was filled with towers of books, newspapers, shopping bags and assorted papers.

Spinster's long life

Vienna, Oct 5.—An Austrian woman who celebrates her 107th birthday on Saturday attributes her longevity to remaining a spinster and working until she was 90.

Car hits police station

Mrs Christine Reeves, a teacher, saw her car run 100 yards downhill and crash into the police station at Dursley, Gloucestershire, yesterday, after she got out to push it. Only the car was damaged.

WAITER! MY WIG IS ON FIRE

A woman who says a waiter set fire to her wig while trying to light a flambé steak Diane is suing Holiday Inns hotels. Nancy Chamberlain, 31, of Pekin, Illinois, seeks personal injury damages of $5,000 (£2,500), and $200 for her brunette wig.

She said the wig, her natural hair, forehead, and eyebrows were scorched by the flames and that she still suffers physical effects of the "embarrassing and painful incident," two years ago at the Holiday Inn, in Des Moines, Iowa, where she stayed on a business trip.

HOW A VICAR LEARNED THE NAKED TRUTH

An anonymous clergyman was annoyed when no one answered his knock at the door of a house, reports the parish magazine at Normanton, Derby.

He left his visiting card, writing on it "Revelation 3, 20. Behold I stand at the door and knock; if anyone hears my voice and opens the door I will come to him."

The next Sunday a woman attended church service and gave the vicar her card inscribed: "Genesis 3: 10" The vicar looked it up and read: "I heard the sound of thee in the garden and I was afraid, because I was naked and hid myself."

Poison sauce kills 20

Abidjan, Ivory Coast, May 2.—Twenty children, aged between two and five years, have died after eating a sauce contaminated by a mouse that had consumed rat poison.

Woman kept 170 cats in flat

Santa Monica, Feb 10.—A critically ill California woman kept 170 dead or dying cats in her one-bedroom flat, placing the dead ones in a makeshift morgue of cardboard boxes. They were found after Miss Patricia Wittlesey was taken to hospital

Mr A. W. McGowan, of the city animal shelter, said 100 dead cats were found stuffed in cardboard boxes stacked to the ceiling, in plastic bags and on top of tables. The 70 surviving cats were half-starved.

SAN FRANCISCO: A Surgeon who performed the world's first testicle transplant says new techniques have been developed to suture blood vessels and other ducts no bigger than the full stop at the end of this sentence.

BURNED SCALP ENDS BALDNESS

Doctors were unable to explain last night why a man bald for 30 years grew a head of hair after his boat blew up. "There is no medical explanation," said Dr John Flood of Trenton, New Jersey.

Mr James Naso, 54, was severley burned over 50 per cent of his body, including his scalp, when his boat exploded on July 1.

Viewers angry over ITN 'rescued cat'

Animal lovers rang up ITN last night to complain about a news item about a cat.

Mr Reginald Bosanquet, the news reader, ended News at Ten with a report about an emergency call from an old lady answered by an Army "Green Goddess" fire appliance in London.

The soldiers, in the last week of their service during the firemen's strike, arrived to rescue her pet cat from a tree and were then invited in for tea.

They accepted gratefully, then left. Unfortunately, according to Mr Bosanquet, they ran over the rescued cat on their way back to their barracks.

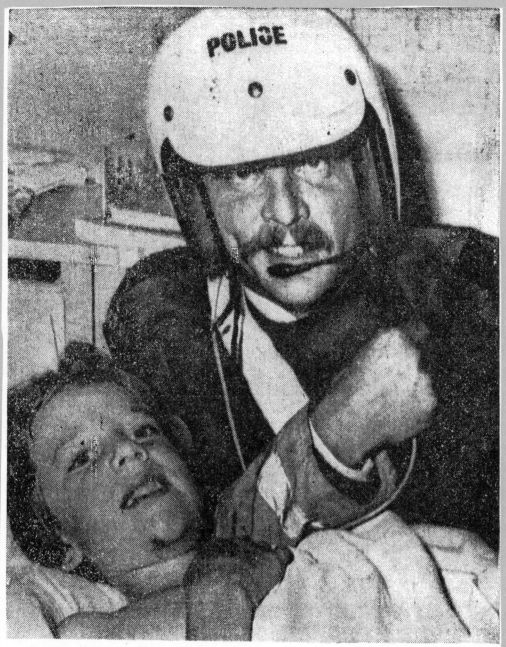

Workmen's mistake left woman foaming

Bristol

Mrs Ann Kelly got a shock when workmen who were injecting insulation foam into the walls of her home drilled into her deep freeze by mistake, but she was even more astonished when they drilled through a lounge wall by mistake and then accidentally filled the central heating system with foam.

The foam started oozing out of joints in pipes in the kitchen and lounge. The workmen said they drilled into the lounge after taking a wrong measurement and also that they had drilled into a wooden box, not realizing it contained central heating pipes.

"I just could not believe it," Mrs Kelly said. "It was impossible to be angry because it was all so funny. And I did not have time to think because I was busy trying to stop the foam coming through. It was like something from outer space when it started coming through the wall in the lounge."

The catalogue of disasters resulted after Mrs Kelly, aged 48, and her husband, decided to have their home at Oakdale Close, Downend, near Bristol, insulated.

They asked a local firm, Zenith, to do the work. Zenith has promised to repair the damage and has sent workmen round to clear up the mess. The firm said it had replaced the deep freeze and would be redecorating the lounge.

PHILLIP Davies, 10, being visited in a Bath hospital yesterday by Pc Steve Scott who helped in a search for the boy's missing front tooth which was knocked out when he was involved in an accident while cycling home.

The tooth was found by an off-duty policeman's mongrel and Pc Scott managed to stop the dog eating it. "I then jumped on my motor cycle with the tooth in my back pocket and hurried off to the hospital," he said.

At the hospital the tooth was put back in place by a dental surgeon and it is hoped the operation will be a success.

Lords' crown falls

A large wooden ornamental crown fell from the ceiling of the Lords last night while peers were debating the Housing Bill. It landed on an unoccupied bench. No one was hurt.

House hunters' grisly find

A 55-year-old woman, was found hanging in her home in Morden Road, Morden last week by two people viewing the house.

Priest dives off cliff to pay debt

Villers le Lac, France

- A 70-year-old retired French priest dived 55ft from a cliff into a river here to pay off a property debt in his former parish.

Abé Robert Simon, curator of Saône near here from 1944 to 1963, was sponsored by parishioners for the dive to the extent of 40,000 francs (£3,300).

Refuse collector

Paris — A 49-year-old bank clerk with a mania for rubbish was found dead in his flat on top of a mountain of empty bottles, rags and waste paper collected in years of rummaging through dustbins and piled only 4ft from the ceiling. Every item had been cleaned before being added to the pile.

Lucky mistake

Dijon — An unemployed man from Dijon won a French record 1,798,328 francs (about £164,000) on a horse-racing bet due to a mistake. In a hurry when he filled in his slip, he accidentally included the number four, which as a rule he avoided because of an "unconditional hatred" for it.

Poor planning

Dr Yvonne Hodges, head of a family planning clinic in Axminster, Devon, has unintentionally become pregnant.

She and her husband, a general practitioner, already have two children. She said: "It just shows we can all make mistakes".

Not so dishy

Seoul — South Korea is to ban the sale of dog meat, snake soup and earthworm soup in the centre of the capital and near tourist hotels because they look disgusting to foreigners. In future these dishes, particularly favoured by stamina building Koreans, will be available only in less conspicuous areas.

Heroin trip

New York — Two Nigerians were arrested at Kennedy airport after they literally tried to walk $2m (£1.3m) worth of heroin, concealed in their shoes, through customs. Their overthick soles gave them away.

Schoolgirl delivered own baby

A girl aged 14 delivered her own baby after concealing her pregnancy from family, friends and teachers. But the boy died immediately, the Southwark coroner was told yesterday.

The girl, who lives in south London, was preparing to go to school when she complained of a stomach ache, the inquest was told. A short time later she gave birth alone in the bathroom. No one had realized the girl's condition.

Recording that the baby died from lack of attention at birth, Sir Montague Levine, the coroner, said: "There is nothing whatsoever to indicate anyone took any active part in killing this baby".

Honey jam

Shreveport, Louisiana About 18 million honey bees escaped when a lorry carrying 720 boxes of them overturned near here. They formed a 40ft-wide swarm over the highway for more than five hours as car windows were rolled up in a six-mile traffic jam and beekeepers lured the swarm back into boxes.

Life-saving hat

Tel Aviv — A hat saved the life of its owner, Mr Simon Korn, aged 69. A doctor was driving behind a bus when he saw a hat blown off a passenger's head. When the owner made no attempt to retrieve it, the doctor stopped the bus and found Mr Korn, the passenger, has suffered a heart attack. He gave him emergency treatment.

Out of the frying pan into . . .

A man acquitted yesterday of shoplifting was arrested as he left the court and was charged with stealing a juror's coat.

Far from home

Jiddah — A thirsty Dutch carrier pigeon found in the desert near here has been returned to the Netherlands.

Burglar, aged 7

Liège — A seven-year-old gipsy boy who entered a house at night after breaking a window was arrested in possession of stolen jewelry. Several houses in the area were burgled recently.

GRANDMOTHER ATTENDS HER OWN 'WAKE'

A 64-year-old grandmother sent out invitations to her own "funeral" party and so many relatives turned up yesterday, including some from Canada, that she had to hire the village hall.

Mrs Christine Farman, of Milton Malsor, Northants, who last attended a family funeral four years ago, said: "Like most families with old members we only seem to meet these days at each other's funerals. So I thought I'd hold my own funeral party while I am still around to enjoy it.

"Now I'll die happy. I haven't met anyone yet who could say they enjoyed their own wake." Mrs Farman's 73-year-old husband, Percy, over-slept. "He's a bit of an eccentric. But he's taking it in the spirit it was intended," she said.

Girl, 13, gives birth at school

A girl, aged 13, was in hospital last night after giving birth between school lessons. An inquiry has started into how she kept her pregnancy secret for so long.

The police were called after the premature baby's dead body was found in the washroom. The girl was later taken from the school in Kingsteignton, Devon, to Torbay Hospital, where her condition last night was said to be satisfactory.

STORK IS GIVEN PLASTIC BEAK

A dentist got his teeth into an unusual job this week—and gave a stork a new beak. Mr Tony Wooton, of Witney, Oxon, was called in by the Cotswold Wildlife Park, Burford, Oxon, when a maribou stork lost threequarters of her lower beak.

After taking an impression Mr Wooton made a beak from toughened plastic used for false teeth and the stork is now eating fish again.

JAIL ESCAPE IN CARDBOARD BOX

A 26-year-old prisoner on remand escaped from a Munich jail by hiding away in a cardboard box destined for an electronics firm.

He hid in a box of metal rods manufactured in the prison workshop. The box was loaded on to a lorry and transported out of the prison without being inspected by guards.

GHOST VILLAGE GETS A RECTOR

The Rev Leslie Wilks, was installed as rector of the Suffolk village of Polstead yesterday, to replace the Rev Hayden Foster, who left the v illage after five nights at the rectory, claiming the building was haunted.

The 16th-century rectory was later sold to Mr John Hayward, a businessman, f or £74,000. The official reason for the sale was that the rectory was too big. Mr Wilks will live in a new house built in the village.

Nearly 300 people have applied to take part in a national plant talking competition organized by a gardening magazine to find Britain's champion plant talker. Finalists will have to bring their favourite plant to a judging in London later this month and talk to it before a panel of experts. The publishers said that half the entries had come from the South-east, and only two from Scotland, where dour Celtic plants are obviously less impressed by sweet talk.

Bodies flown out as mass suicide toll is put at 912

Washington, Nov 26

American troops have removed all the bodies from the jungle settlement of Jonestown in Guyana, and the final aircraft load of some 180 bodies was arriving in the United States today.

The final death toll in the mass suicide which took place a week ago after the shooting of an American Congressman and four other Americans is estimated to be 912, including some 260 children.

Only about 80 members of the People's Temple cult in Guyana appear to have escaped death—32 of them from the settlement itself and another 46 based in Georgetown, the capital of Guyana.

Two of the survivors have been formally charged with murder by the Guyanese authorities. The remainder are expected to be allowed to return to the United States.

Gentlemen lift the seat

LIFE in West Africa can be pretty hazardous, what with pirates, the appalling climate and the necessity to even bribe the policeman on point duty. In Nigeria, where a fair amount of the communications depend upon fast watercraft, entirely new hazards are to be encountered. The speedboat drivers are renowned for their love of a full throttle, a full bottle and a complete lack of water sense that has apparently to be experienced to be appreciated. We heard of one sad case where a couple of classificiation society surveyors, sitting thoughtfully in the stern as their boat rushed through the Niger delta were flung bodily into the water as their driver bounced his water taxi over a large log and roared off without even noticing their absence, leaving them to swim for it.

On another occasion one of the Rotork Sea Trucks, fast flat bottomed workboats shaped like small landing craft was speeding up a creek in the same area when its driver and sole occupant urgently felt the call of nature. Most prudent seamen would have at least throttled back or hove to, but this single minded person was squatting over the stern when the craft left the river at an estimated speed of 25 knots. It then passed a large palm tree, leaving it to both port and starboard as the craft was sliced in two like a cheese. The driver, who doubtless was making a note to eat milder curries in future, was flung right over the top of the cabin roof to land on the nearly bisected foredeck, breaking a leg. And serve him right.

572lb sturgeon

Sofia, Nov 16.—Fishermen in the village of Kosaya caught in the Danube a 572lb sturgeon estimated to be 80 to 100 years old and yielding 97lb of caviar.

WORKERS GIVEN SUNNY DAYS OFF

The head of Oslo's Public Health department has told his 950 staff they can take the day off when the sun shines, and make up time later.

Dr Fredrik Mallbye says they should be able to enjoy the sunshine after an exceptionally rainy summer. The offer applies to the autumn only.

Secret weapon

Bonn, Dec 5.—West Germany's defence budget for 1979 includes the cost of a gold tooth for Alf, an alsatian guard dog at Fassberg airbase.

Baby's high speed delivery

TOKYO, Thursday. A NEW BORN BABY who fell from a moving train was today "doing fine," crying and drinking milk at the Japan Red Cross medical centre.

A 44-year-old woman lost consciousness and dropped the 6lb 9oz baby boy down the lavatory hole after going into labour and giving birth on a commuter train travelling at about 30 miles an hour.

The baby was found on the track 5 hours later, after seven trains had passed over him. Railway workers began the search after the woman regained consciousness at a hospital and told police that she thought she had given birth.

Normal

Dr Hiroshi Akamatsu said at the medical centre that the baby suffered an L-shaped crack in the scalp and an injury on the head that required four stitches.

He said the child showed signs of improving and was a normal healthy infant as for respect to pulse, respiration and temperatude goes.

"The boy cries and drinks milk," he said.

The baby was still in a serious condition, the doctor said, and he could not tell immediately how long it would be before it could be allowed home.

The hospital in Takasaki, near Tokyo, where the woman was being treated said she was in a satisfactory condition but was still nervous about the baby, her fourth child.

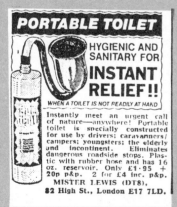

Grandmother at 28

Messina, Sicily, Nov 24.— Angela Sarao became a grandmother at the age of 28 today when her 14-year-old daughter gave birth here. Mrs Sarao was herself a mother at 14.

A cyclists nightmare. This multi-bike pile up in Chaud-des-Fonds on the Tour de France was caused by a dog running across the road in front of the riders.

Woman was found to be alive in coffin

Gloucester

A woman certified dead from a drugs overdose came back to life in a mortuary yesterday.

She had been found at her home in Chapel Street, Stroud, early yesterday morning. A doctor certified death and an undertaker took her to the Gloucester mortuary.

Mr David Faulkner, the Cheltenham district coroner, said: "A death was reported to me in the usual way and in accordance with standard procedures I gave authority for the body to be removed to the mortuary. It is a most unfortunate incident.

Bokassa cook says he fried human flesh

Bangui, Dec 22.—A palace cook of former Emperor Bokassa told a court here in the Central African Republic today that he fried human flesh for the deposed monarch.

Apology rejected

Houston, Texas. — A woman fired at her former husband when he visited a hospital here to apologize for shooting her in the head. Police said he ran from the premises saying, "She missed again, she missed again".

Bokassa's crocodiles 'ate his enemies'

AUTHORITIES investigating charges of cannibalism and mass killings against deposed Emperor Bokassa reported last night that they had recovered the remains of nearly 40 bodies from a crocodile pool behind one of his residences.

It is assumed that Bokassa used the crocodiles to execute his enemies.

Only large bones were found. Crocodiles eat smaller ones. The pool was drained following Bokassa's overthrow.

It was in a cold room in the same residence, in the outskirts of Bangui, where last week authorities found three dismembered human bodies, adding to intense speculation about the deposed dictator's alleged activities as a cannibal.

Officials said last night that they are trying to establish the identity of the victims found in the crocodile pool while a search is going on for further proof that Bokassa was a cannibal.

Yesterday, a young girl arrived at her convent school in Bangui and told teachers she was absent last week because her family was in mourning for her uncle "who was eaten by Bokassa."

It is widely held in Bangui that guests at Bokassa's coronation banquet were served human flesh.

Up to 15 years ago, human flesh was on sale in the public market in Bangui. Missionaries practised in the country.

Bokassa's own tribe, the M'paka, are known cannibals, and on this basis alone it is more than likely that Bokassa was a practising cannibal.

Choice cuts

The idea behind cannibalism in Central Africa is that the consumer eats parts of an enemy's pobdy in the belief that he absorbs the quality of his enemy. Most favoured portions are the brains, heart and genitals.

Most cannibalism in the country is of a ritual nature. Sometimes those who die normally are subsequently eaten.

It is a mistaken belief in Europe that cannibalism has been largely eradicated in Africa. Missionaries believe that it is still widespread.

Shark dies in attack on anglers

Portsmouth

A 400lb shark was killed yesterday as it leapt at a small fishing boat off the south coast. Two fishermen were injured and the boat was damaged when the shark landed across the deck.

The incident happened off the Isle of Wight. Mr Ross Staplehurst, a local fisherman, had taken a party of anglers for a day's fishing in his 23ft boat, the Albatross. They were fishing for tope and skate when the thresher shark, 13 ft long, was sighted about 50 yards away.

Mr Staplehurst said: "It turned towards the boat and dived. Everything was quiet for a moment and we thought it had swum away. Then there was a great rushing noise and suddenly the shark came surging out of the water about five yards away.

"It landed across the boat, which is only 9ft wide, so its head and tail were sticking over each end. The impact nearly sank the boat and it killed the shark outright."

One of the fishermen was hit by the shark's tail and his nose was cut. Another had a bruised leg. The Albatross sailed back to Bembridge, Isle of Wight, where the shark is to be sold to fishmongers.

Mr Staplehurst said: "I have fished these waters for 10 years but have never seen a shark act like this. It just went berserk. I'm convinced it was attacking the boat."

RAT-ATOUILLE

Rats are being bred for food in Ghana, Nigeria, and the Ivory Coast. South African radio reported yesterday. It said 500 farmers were increasing giant and cave rat populations to provide alternative meat sources.

Driver's dim view

A Suffolk motorist whose car headlights failed on Saturday smashed his windscreen and both headlamps and jumped on the bonnet. Police arrived as he was attempting to wrench off the doors.

Sausage killing

Wellington — Malcolm Francis, aged 35, is standing trial in Napier, New Zealand, on a charge of beating his wife to death with a frozen sausage. He has denied murder.

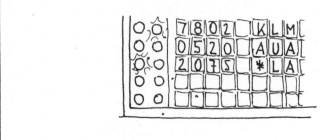

Heathrow fights invasion of fleas

The British Airports Authority has launched an offensive against an invasion of fleas at Heathrow. The fleas have infested departure lounge carpets and are said to have been breeding in luggage X-ray scanning machines.

Dozens of passengers and staff have complained of bites. The authority said some had been treated in a medical centre; but they were confident a pest control company had overcome the problem.

Those trousers turn up again—set in concrete

THE moleskin trousers which Roy Collette and his brother-in-law Larry Kunkle have sent each other for Christmas for the past 12 years, have turned up again.

This time, they arrived at Larry's home in Illinois, curled inside a 6ft. high-abrasion tyre filled with three tons of concrete.

The tyre, guaranteed uncuttable' by its makers, was delivered by truck and neatly tied with a ribbon.

Last year, Larry sent them to Roy in Minneapolis in the glove-box of a car which had been crushed into a 3ft. cube. The year before that Roy sent the same trousers welded inside a 600lb safe bound with reinforced steel bars.

Every year the wrapping becomes more difficult. The challenge is to unwrap them in time for the next Christmas.

'Getting the trousers out of the squashed car was the most miserable job of my life,' said Roy. 'I finally managed it with the help of a carbide saw, blow torch, air chisel and a lot of blood, sweat and tears.'

Monkey business

Jakarta, Nov 29.—Officials in the central Celebes area of Indonesia are considering importing monkeys for training as coconut pickers.

Runaway bull captured in third-floor flat

Madrid, Feb 14.—Police, firemen and dozens of passers by in the northern town of Zamora today joined in an impromptu bullfight that ended two hours later with the capture of the animal in a third-floor flat.

The bull tore loose after being tied to a tree near the cattle market. After damaging a car, it entered a building, smashed down doors and partitions.

Helped by police and firemen, the owner's nephew managed to throw a rope around the animal's neck. The rope was tied to a lorry which dragged the bull out.

The silent guest

Santiago, May 3.—The three-day party in a Santiago suburb was noisy enough to wake the dead, but it did not disturb José Luís Huenchupan, who was sitting quietly in the corner. He died on the first day and none of his fellow guests noticed.

Medal for dog

Emma, a guide dog which went blind and has to be led around by another guide dog, won the gold medal for devotion to duty at a dinner held in London yesterday. Emma is owned by Miss Sheila Hocken, of Nottingham.

SMOKING 'NUN' WAS WEARING BROWN BOOTS

A policeman became suspicious when he noticed a nun wearing brown boots and smoking a cigarette, magistrates at Wakefield, West Yorks, heard yesterday.

Roger Clifton, of Portalon Street, Wakefield, and his sister Louise, 17, of Pledwick Lane, Wakefield, admitted conduct likely to cause a breach of the peace and both were bound over for two years.

They admitted dressing as nuns to attend a Wakefield Trinity rugby league game. Mr Wilson Jackson, chairman of the bench, told them: "You could have caused a riot."

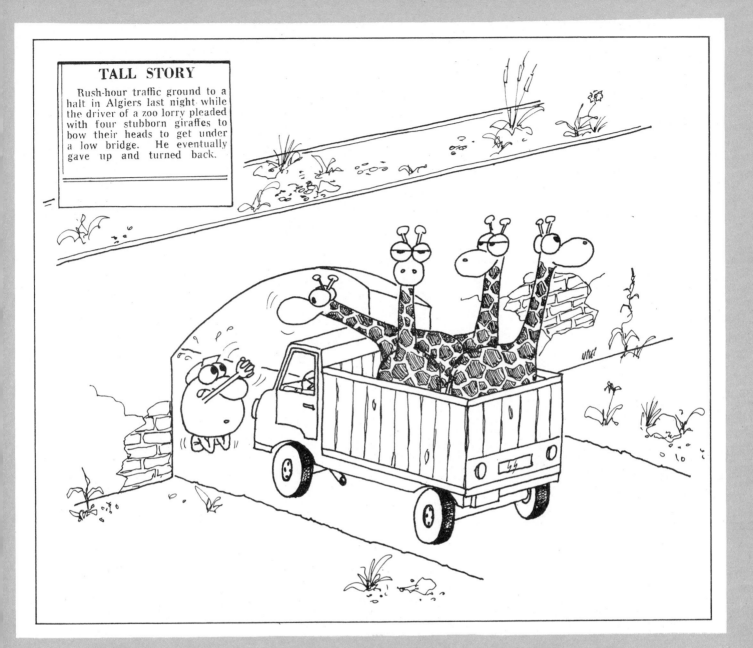

STOWAWAY CAT CHANGED PLANE FOR LONDON

Airline officials are mystified as to how a stowaway Siamese cat which travelled from a tiny Pacific island to London via Washington managed to change aircraft by itself.

Wanton Bacon, identified by a collar tag, was flown back yesterday to his owners, an American naval family based at Guam, after airline staff at Heathrow found him in the hold of a jumbo jet.

A Pan American official said: " We think it must have walked across the tarmac and jumped on the aWshington flight. Then itm ust have changed planes at Washington Airport for a London flight. The cat sounds almost bionic."

TWO-HEADED BABY

A girl with two heads and three arms has been born in a New Delhi hospital. Doctors, who would not comment on her condition, said she had two nervous systems, but one heart. One hand has eight fingers.

Bowler breaks thief's arm

Bogata, Nov 7.—A 16-year-old pick'ocket tried to snatch awrist watch from Tom Marshall the British bowling champion, on his way to the opening session of the bowling world cup.

Marshall, from Cranford, Middlesex, felt his watch strap being tugged from Behind. He wheeled round, snatched the thief's arm and cracked it over his knee.

A stitch in time
saves arm

A Turkish seaman left a hospital in Cleveland after an operation which saved his right arm.

Mr David Muckle, surgeon at Middlesbrough General Hospital, stitched Ismet Ince's arm back on 4½ hours after it was severed in an accident aboard a tanker in the North Sea last January.

" He should have 70 per cent. use of his arm," said Mr Muckle.

SEVEN SUFFOCATED

Seven people died of suffocation near Ahmedabad in India when a man fell into a cow dung pit and six jumped in to try to rescue him. Dung plants produce fertilisers and gas for cooking and lighting in Indian villages.

Naples relieved as saint's blood liquefies

Rome, Sept 19

Relief today greeted the announcement in Naples that the substance said to be the blood of St Januarius, patron of the city, had liquefied as usual on the anniversary of his decapitation.

The crowds in the cathedral where the flask containing the substance is kept were also told that the stone on which the saint's head was placed after his death went a noticeable pink.

A failure to liquefy is normally regarded as a very bad omen for Naples. The relief is natural given the tension in the city where unemployment is now stated to be reaching levels dangerous to public order.

Woman of 93 hit cabbie with her walking stick

Miami, Nov 30.—A 93-year-old woman was jailed here for a night on a charge of armed robbery after she refused to pay what she considered an exorbitant taxi fare, then hit the driver with her walking stick and fought police who came to his aid.

Johanna Briscoe refused to pay the $10 (about £5) fare on Friday. When the taxi-driver protested, she hit him with her walking stick.

When the caretakers of the flats where she lives came to his aid, she attacked them too. Two policemen who came to investigate were kicked, scratched and hit with the stick.

After finally overpowering the woman, they charged her with armed robbery and resisting arrest, " disarmed " her and took her off to prison.

Back at home, she was reported to have recovered with the aid of a large whisky and orange juice.

Sign of trouble—an electronic protest when a car made a forced entry at a bank after careering off a State highway in eastern Missouri.

Forced silence in court

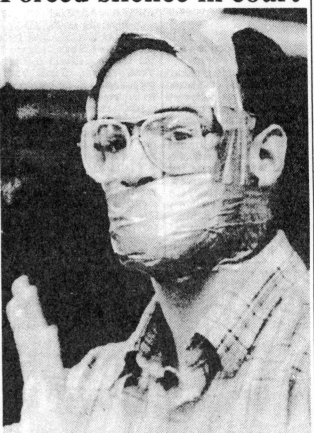

Christopher Masters, aged 22, gagged with a sanitary napkin and tape for refusing to be quiet at a pre-trial hearing in Houston, Texas.

When the gag was removed yesterday, Mr Masters sat quietly in court and did not say a word. He was gagged at first with a man's tie, but he tore it off and continued to berate his lawyer, the judge and the prosecutor. The judge finally ordered that he be gagged more effectively.

Top cyclist keeps going despite laxative plot

U-turn driver fined

Basingstoke magistrates fined Miss Enid Martin, aged 82, of Briantspuddle, Dorset, a total of £100 yesterday after she admitted making two U-turns and driving the wrong way on the M3 south of Basingstoke.

£8,000 ache

Manila — A court ordered two surgeons to pay about £8,000 in damages for leaving a 5in pair of forceps in a patient's stomach for over two years. The man had complained of stomach ache.

On the cross

Warsaw — A Polish village carpenter murdered a 76-year-old customer and then nailed his body to a cross which he erected in a field, according to a newspaper report here. The carpenter had spent two periods in a mental hospital.

Bad timing

Tiberias — An 83-year-old man here allowed police to destroy a suspiciously ticking package, only to learn it contained a gold watch, his reward for banking 40 years at the National Bank of Israel.

Pasta hijack

Hongkong — The hijacking of a lorry containing 950 boxes of spaghetti, 350 bags of macaroni and 760 bags of flour from Japan, has left Italian restaurants seriously short of supplies.

Thief returned for other shoe

A pre-Christmas shoplifter, who found he had stolen two left shoes, was arrested the next day while taking a matching right shoe.

CHOCOLATE ART GOES DOWN WELL

A sculpture, made of chocolate, has been getting smaller and smaller during a tour of northern art galleries as parties of schoolchildren snip off pieces to eat while their teachers are not looking.

A spokesman for the York-based chocolate firm Rowntree Mackintosh who sponsor Colin Wilbourn's work, said yesterday the firm was having to use the sculpture's original mould to cast a new chocolate exhibit for each gallery it visited.

Dog tragedy

Nairobi, — A villager leapt into a 25ft deep latrine pit to rescue his dog despite seeing a cobra inside. The reptile attacked and bit him before he cut it in half and emerged with the dog. But the snake bite proved fatal. His relatives killed the dog in their anger.

SOS from wardrobe

An RAF air-sea rescue helicopter searched the Firth of Clyde yesterday and vessels in the area were alerted in a hunt for what turned out to be a distress call from a Renfrewshire council house.

Mr and Mrs Leslie Brown, of Erskine, had bought a faulty distress beacon for their sailing boat. They were asleep when it started broadcasting from the top of their wardrobe and the signal was picked up by a Soviet search and rescue satellite over the North Atlantic.

Oldest prisoner

New York — A man who says he is 96 and has a criminal record dating back to 1929 has been sentenced to six months in jail for trying to swindle at least seven women.

Growing pain

Mr Ken Wood of Tavistock, Devon, is to sell his £11,500 custom-built Morgan sports car, after waiting seven years for delivery, because he has gained two stone in weight and cannot get into the car.

Surefire hit at the bank

A BANK in Illinois is giving two revolvers to anyone who opens an account with £1500.
Eight hundred people have already taken up the offer. A bank official said : " Instead of us handing over money to people with guns it's the other way round."

Trapped girls saved

Three teenage girl laundry workers were rescued by firemen yesterday after being locked in a lavatory for 12 hours at Raynors underwear factory in Nottingham. They thought they heard a burglar and fled into the lavatory for safety but the catch was faulty and the door jammed shut.

250 dead cats found

Toulouse, March 22.—The remains of nearly 250 cats neatly stacked in shoe boxes were found in the basement of the home of a woman teacher who died a year ago, aged 84. She ministered especially to terminally-ill animals.

Runway body

Frankfurt — An American man whose body was found next to a Frankfurt airport runway appears to have been a stowaway who froze to death in the landing gear compartment during a transatlantic flight.

Mother, aged 10

Houston — A 10-year-old girl who gave birth to a baby last week and the child were both in satisfactory condition yesterday, hospital officials said.

Inside story

Jakarta — Fishermen at Labuan Lombok in eastern Indonesia, slicing up a 9ft shark they had netted, discovered a human skeleton inside.

Poisonous delivery

Nicholls, Georgia — Mr James Carter has been charged with sending a poisonous rattlesnake through the mail to Mr Joey Tanner.

The local District Attorney commented: "I think it would be safe to say Mr Carter didn't care for Mr Tanner". Mr Tanner killed the snake with a hoe.

D-I-Y flight attendant grounded

New York

A MAN who flew around the world for two years posing as a Pan American flight attendant was grounded yesterday—after playing his role too well.

Police in Miami charged William Cohn, 31, with stealing £25.000 from the airline. The flights, they said, had taken him as far afield as London, Hongkong, Honolulu, Johannesburg and Abidjan.

Cohn told police that he had trained as a flight attendant in 1972 but was never hired by the airline. He dropped out of the training programme to go to college.

But he was able to acquire an attendant's uniform. Wearing this, he was waved on to aircraft by security staff, and cabin crew checking tickets never questioned him.

Passengers' praise

Once abroad, he would tell the genuine attendants that he was travelling on company business, and usually offered to help on the flight.

Passengers were so impressed with his efficiency and courtesy that a number wrote letters of commendation to the airline. When Pan Am's personnel department tried to put the letters on his file, they found he didn't have one.

Police and airport security officials were alerted, and Cohn was arrested at Pan Am's Miami office when he tried to exchange some airline tickets.

Scores of birds die in suicide attacks on homes

Belgrade — Scores of birds killed themselves this week by crashing into houses in Zabljak, Yugoslavia's highest town in Montenegro.

The birds beat window panes with their beaks or with their wings in scenes resembling the Hitchcock horror film *The Birds*.

Twenty-two birds died when they crashed through an open window into the bathtub of Micun Karadzic.

GARDEN OIL WELL

Jakarta, May 22.—A workman repairing a fence in a woman's garden in Lampaseh Kota, northern Indonesia, dug a hole and struck oil. It gushed out of the flower beds and triggered a minor " black gold " rush by neighbours and the state oil company.

Dwarf protest stops contest

Bonn — An international dwarf-throwing competition in West Germany next month involving a British group, the Oddballs with a 4ft 4in man called Lenny the Giant, has been cancelled after protests from small people. The organizer said he had called it off after receiving complaints from people of restricted growth in West Germany, Britain and The Netherlands.

Dustbin catch of porcupine

A runaway porcupine was captured in Carshalton, Surrey, yesterday by a policeman who trapped it in a dustbin. Constable James Havall had earlier tried to catch the animal in a cardboard box, but it ate it. Last night the porcupine was in quarantine at Chessington Zoo, waiting for someone to claim it.

Porcupines are vegetarian, and shoot their quills when threatened.

MAN KILLED FRIGID WIFE

A man whose wife had agreed to have sexual intercourse only once in eight years plotted to strangle her into unconsciousness so he could have sex, Leeds Crown Court was told yesterday. But he went too far and she died.
" The only time we had sex our five-year-old daughter Kerry was conceived."

CAUGHT NAPPING

An intruder who drank a can of beer in the offices of a Nottingham building supply firm fell asleep in an armchair, and was still sleeping soundly when the cleaner arrived yesterday morning. He was later arrested.

Security breach

Hongkong, June 24.—A 28-year-old burglar has been jailed for six months for stealing from the colony's Secretary for Security, who was injured in the raid—not by the burglar, but by his wife, who swung a golf club at the intruder and missed.

President Amin ' ate liver of dead minister '

President Amin of Uganda ate part of the liver of a dead minister in an attempt to keep away evil spirits, a former personal physician to the President said in London last night.

Professor John Kibukamusoke, a Ugandan, now professor of medicine at Zambia University in Lusaka, told a meeting of the Africa Bureau at the Commons that the liver came from Mr Michael Ondaga, the Ugandan Foreign Minister, whose body was found floating in the Nile in 1973.

Professor Kibukamusoke, personal physician to President Amin from 1971 to 1973 when he fled the country, said the President was very superstitious and believed strongly that " if you eat a piece of your victim's liver his evil spirits will not haunt you ".

He said the liver had found its way to President Amin's command post and part of it was eaten by the President.

He said President Amin suffered from hypomania—which was a flight of ideas.

Iceland manhunt

Reykjavik — Police cordoned off a large area of Reykjavik in a hunt for a gunman who carried out the first armed robbery in Iceland's history when he fled with 2m crowns (about £48,500) taken from two messengers about to deposit it in the National Bank of Iceland.

ICE-LOLLIES FOR ESKIMOS

A Danish firm is to ship 50,000 do-it-yourself lice-lollies to Greenland. "Greenlanders can mix them and put them in refrigerators or, for most of the year, can just leave them out of doors to freeze," a spokesman said.

Firm friends separated

Suzanne Watts, whose left hand became stuck to her friend Lynda Gartam's right hand when they were using a powerful glue, prised their hands apart at home yesterday after doctors at Stroud General Hospital, Gloucestershire, had failed to separate them. The girls live at Rodborough.

GOLDEN THUMB

Relatives of an illiterate man cut off his thumb after he died, preserved it in formaldehyde and used it to endorse and cash his pension cheques, an inquiry in Toronto was told yesterday. The swindle worked for years before it was detected during a routine survey of pensioners.

Lamp post stops freedom break

Two prisoners in their early twenties broke out of Swansea Magistrates' Court yesterday and ran either side of a lamp post, forgetting they were handcuffed together and breaking their wrists. They were treated in hospital.

Later they were remanded in custody for a week. Their names were not disclosed to prevent their case being prejudiced.

Spinsters lived with dead mother

Paris, Aug 13

In the little town of Sanary-sur-Mer in the Var lived, so their neighbours thought, two devoted spinster daughters. Although their mother was over 90 and too ill to go out, they both stayed at home to look after her.

This week, however, they found out just how the two sisters were looking after their mother. The discovery followed the attempt by a local town hall official to deliver a letter addressed to the mother, Mme Helene Barbaroux.

No matter how hard he tried he found he could not get past the two daughters, Jeanne and Genevieve, who told him through the barely open door that their mother was too ill to see him and was, in fact, being treated by the doctor.

The town hall official became suspicious. The doctor they mentioned had been dead to his certain knowledge for the past six years. He went to the police who obtained a warrant and went to call on Mme Barbaroux.

The two sisters would not let the police in. Eventually they called in the fire brigade and the door was forced open.

Inside they found Mme Barbaroux wrapped in a coat. She had been dead for the past three or four years. It was impossible to tell exactly how long.

For all that time the sisters had kept their mother's death a secret and used to move her about the house wrapped in the coat whenever it was necessary to hide her from a visitor. The elder sister, aged 63, usually slept with her mother's body on the bed beside her.

By keeping the death a secret the two sisters were able to continue to draw their mother's pension, which although small, made a great difference to their meagre incomes.

Tortoise freed

Nairobi.—A tortoise suspected of causing the deaths of six people in Kyuasini village, in the Machakos district of Kenya's Eastern Province, was sentenced to death but then chained to a tree when no one could be found to execute it. The district officer persuaded them to free it on the promise of an official inquiry into the deaths.

Manic squirrel

A fighting-mad squirrel which has bitten six victims in less than four weeks is terrorizing villagers in East Bridgford, Nottinghamshire. They have called in Rushford Borough Council's pest control officer to find it.

Police, firemen and doctors can't budge 52-stone woman

DEFIANT 52-stone Mrs Muriel Hopkins refuses to go to hospital. Doctors, alarmed at her condition, want her in hospital for urgent treatment to lose weight.

"I am definitely not going — I prefer to be with my mum," she said yesterday.

"They will only stop me smoking and starve me to death."

Mrs Hopkins, 48, is so heavy that she is unable to walk and spends most of her day trapped in a chair at her mother's home.

An ambulance crew called to take Mrs Hopkins to Dudley Hospital, but she was too heavy to move. The fire brigade came to help. But Mrs Hopkins became fed up with the attempts and refused to go.

Now doctors will make regular visits to see if Mrs Hopkins can respond to treatment at her mother's home and health visitors will keep a wtchful eye on her.

Mrs Hopkins, who lives in Tipton, went to stay with her 85-year-old mother over Easter. She fell just over a week ago and police and firemen were called in to get her upright.

Mrs Beatrice Brown, her mother, cannot walk without the aid of a frame and Mrs Hopkins is being cared for by a home help.

She was sleeping on a temporary bed put up for her on the ground floor of her mother's home, but now she sleeps in a chair because she cannot bend down to get into bed.

Mrs Brown said her daughter had had a weight problem since she was six. She was concerned about her health.

Mrs Hopkins said: "I've always had a weight problem and I smoke like a chimney — 20 a day."

Innocent passion

Lusaka.—A woman who bit off the tip of her lover's tongue during a passionate kiss was cleared by a Lusaka magistrate of causing grievous bodily harm.

Rat-a-tat-tat

Los Angeles — A 52-year-old man has been charged with violating Californian health and safety laws after the discovery of 50 pet rats at his home. A policeman who went to the Los Angeles house said the rats were gnawing the building away.

Fatal falls

Jakarta, Nov 24.—At least 26 people, most of them middle-aged women, plunged to their deaths in east Java yesterday in a scramble to reach a waterfall they believed had the power to restore youth.

Unbridled passion killed bull, court told

A night among a herd of stray cattle transformed Arab, a prize bull from "a magnificent speciment to a total wreck" which had to be destroyed, it was claimed at the High Court at Chester yesterday.

VINTAGE ROBBERY

Burglars who broke into a house in Aachen, West Germany, left a note for the owner saying: "financially a dead loss, but your wine is fantastic Cheers," according to police.

Tomato extract

Stockholm – A dentist in Karlskrona found a sprouting tomato seed embedded in the gum of a 60-year-old male patient. He cut it out and transplanted it to a plant pot, but the seedling was damaged and died.

Budgie eaten

Sydney — Lee Stubbs aged 24, who bit off and chewed a budgerigar's head at a talent contest watched by 200 people at the Maroubra Seals Club was fined $A500 (£294). "It was a spur-of-the-moment action." he told the court.

Limb transplantation will become possible in the next century, surgeon says

Aylesbury

In the next century surgeons will be able to transplant limbs from one body to another, a conference on the techniques of microsurgery was told yesterday. Mr Bruce Bailey, a consultant plastic surgeon at Stoke Mandeville Hospital, Aylesbury, said the techniques for such operations already existed, but tissue rejection had still to be overcome.

LIGHTNING IN PLANE

Ball lightning passed through a Soviet Ilyushin-18 airliner without causing major damage, the Tass agency reported yesterday. A fireball about 4in across went over the heads of passengers when the plane was at about 3.000ft. after leaving Sochi, on the Black Sea.

Topless leap

Four topless women parachutists from Swansea plan to make their descent over the Gower coastline on August Bank holiday Monday to help to raise £30,000 for local hospital breast scanner

Swan's praises sung

Lancelot, the Bewick swan, has set a record by arriving at the Wildfowl Trust, Slimbridge, Gloucestershire, for the eighteenth consecutive winter. The trust believes that he has flown 140,000 miles in migration flights.

Jet-age compensation

Mrs Sandra Pugh has been paid £10 compensation by the Ministry of Defence after a low-flying RAF jet splashed four shirts hanging on the washing line at her home in Callow Hill, Bewdley, Worcester, with an oily fluid.

Easter victim

Nairobi — Kenyan police arrested the parents of a young girl and one other person after interrupting a Good Friday ceremony in which the girl was about to be nailed to a cross.

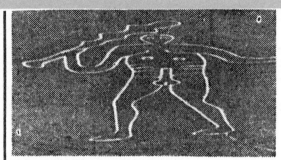

Waiting for a mate: Cerne Giant

Will Marilyn join the Giant in chalky bedrock?

Marilyn Monroe: the famous pose

HILL figures are nothing new at Cerne Abbas. Carved on the downland turf just outside this Dorset village is Britain's oldest full-frontal male nude, the celebrated Cerne Giant, who has preserved his remarkably explicit chalky outline for almost 2,000 years. Now the lusty giant, believed to have been a Romano-British fertility figure, is likely to be joined by a sex symbol from the 20th century.

Ken Evans-Loude, a 33-year-old artist from Kings Nympton in Devon, wants to create a giant chalk figure of Marilyn Monroe on a neighbouring hillside.

What he has in mind for the Dorset downs is a 230ft.-tall Marilyn, skirts flying, chalky limbs bared to the winds in a famous pose from The Seven Year Itch. "To me she is the world. "To me she is the archetypal figure of the 20th century; an international fertility symbol representing the basic needs of our times."

Pure chance led him to Cerne Abbas, says Evans-Loude. He had asked the Ministry of Defence for permission to put Marilyn on the gunnery range near Lulworth but was turned down so he wrote to the Dorset Evening Echo about his plan.

Ian Cobbold, a Cerne Abbas farmer, read his plea and offered him a hillside in full view of the giant. "I couldn't believe my luck when I discovered the two sites were so close," says Evans-Loude. "My Marilyn will give a sense of continuity to Britain's unique tradition of chalkhill figures which goes back thousands of years."

There are problems. The site is bumpy. A fox has dug its lair on the spot destined to become the Monroe navel. The chalk of this hillside is buried under a deep layer of clay, which could mean having to bring chalk to the site, a costly operation.

And then there are the planners — something the giant's creator did not have to contend with. Cobbold argues that a likeness of Marilyn Monroe would not alter the hill's shape and no building or change of land use is envisaged. His sheep would still be there, nibbling around Marilyn's contours. "We've looked very closely at the planning regulations," he says, "and I don't think we need permission." But if they do fall foul of the planners, says Cobbold, "we'll do her in daffodils."

Special delivery

Karachi — Doctors used a motor cycle headlight to deliver a baby at the state-owned Jinnah Hospital during a power failure. The baby girl and her mother are doing well.

Sale is a dead loss

There was no buyer for the former Crewe mortuary when it was offered for sale by auction at Crewe yesterday.

Thief swops glass for big diamond

Sydney, Oct 19.—Australia's biggest diamond was stolen from a jewelry exhibition here yesterday.

The diamond, valued at £250,000, was apparently stolen yesterday by a man posing as a workman who put a piece of cut-glass in its place. The jewel once belonged to the Sultans of Turkey.

Marilyn's lost roses

LOS ANGELES, Thursday: Joe Dimaggio, who was married for three years to Marilyn Monroe, has ended a 20-year standing order for thrice-weekly delivery of roses to her crypt.

Bob Alhanati, a co-owner of the Hollywood florists that has filled the order since Marilyn's drug overdose death in 1962, said Dimaggio gave no explanation for discontinuing the order.

The case of the poison pudding

Kempen, West Germany – Police here believe they have uncovered a real life Agatha Christie plot in which a pensioner murdered two husbands and a lover with poison in their favourite dessert: her home-made pudding.

Frau Maria Velten, aged 67, had a previous conviction for poisoning local cats. Now police believe that was a rehearsal for more serious things to come.

Married by mother

Miss Lynn Montgomery, aged 21, a bank clerk, was married yesterday to Mr Nigel Dymond, aged 22, a radiographer, in a ceremony conducted by her mother, Mrs Trudie Montgomery, superintendent registrar at Sleaford, Lincolnshire.

Wife strangled

Belgrade   A retired policeman who strangled his wife when she tried to stop him watching a World Cup football match on television has been jailed for eight years, Yugoslav newspapers report.

Tickling ban sticks

Nottingham's Goose Fair opened yesterday with a council ban on tickling sticks, or canes with feathers on the end, still in force. It was imposed in 1967 after an incident involving a girl in a miniskirt.

Cows found drunk on sugarbeet

Mr Albert Priday, a Gloucestershire farmer, is double checking his cows' diet after they got drunk from eating too much sugarbeet.

Mr Priday, of Hartledge Hill, Redmarley, found 18 of his heffers lying in a field and at first he thought they had been struck by a virus. But the amimal's breath smelt of alcohol and the cows were simply drunk and incapable.

"I found that instead of a mixture of sugarbeet and hay they had been leaving the hay. The beet would turn into a fruity pulp which fermented in their stomachs. Their knees had gone and they were just like drunken humans, even their eyes were glazed", Mr Priday said.

● Least sucessful hunter: This must be the New Zealander who came off worse after his encounter with a duck that did not take kindly to being shot at. After he had loosed off both barrels of his shotgun at the duck, it circled him and then dive-bombed. It flew straight into his face, breaking his nose, glasses and a tooth.

Two women save girl in struggle with crocodile

Nairobi   – A girl aged 10 was rescued from a crocodile by her father's two wives, the Kenya News Agency reported yesterday.

The girl's mother, Mrs Esha Wako, was fetching water from the Tana river in south-east Kenya last week when she saw the crocodile carrying her daughter, Samaha, into the river. She grabbed the girl's leg and had a tug-of-war with the crocodile, which was gripping the child's buttocks.

Mrs Anja Wako, the second wife of Mr Wako Habudi, heard shouting, plunged into the river and jabbed the crocodile in its eyes. It released the girl and fled.

Samaha received stitches on her buttocks at a clinic and was allowed home.

Rose given as rent for village school

Susan Whittaker, aged 10, presented Princess Alice Duchess of Gloucester with a single rose at Barnwell Manor, Northamptonshire, yesterday as a token payment for the annual rent of the village junior school.

The custom dates to the seventeenth century and was restored by Mr John Parkes, the school's headmaster, after a lapse of 150 years.

Decree for wife aged 73 who was denied sex

A woman aged 73 whose husband, a retired naval officer, turned his back on sex, was granted a decree nisi in the High Court yesterday.

Foot fetishist

Bonn – A 17-year-old youth went on trial in Kiel accused of stabbing a woman and trying to cut off her foot and eat it. The prosecution said his attack came after he had watched a video film about cannibalism.

Award for bitten policeman

Off-duty Police Sergeant Peter Dewer nearly had his eye bitten from its socket when he tried to stop youths brawling outside a public house, it was disclosed yesterday. One of the youths attacked him, biting and tearing the skin beneath his eye and causing the eyeball to fall forward on to his face.

As the youths were arrested after the incident in Yeovil, Somerset the policeman was taken to hospital where surgeons battled to save the sight of his left eye. Sergeant Dewar, aged 41, had two operations in which surgeons restored his sight almost fully.

Motor runs on a lemon for five months

Mr Anthony Ashill, a watch repairer of Kidderminster, Hereford-Worchester, has managed to keep a small electric motor running day and night for the past five months powered by a single lemon.

"I connected two wires to a lemon with a piece of copper and a piece of zinc and soldered them on to the motor. Although the lemon is now black and shrivelled the motor is still going strong.

"If I can make my small motor run for month after month on a single lemon, just imagine how much "juice" there must be in a whole sackful", Mr Ashill said.

Lemon-powered motor spinning on after a year

An electric motor that began spinning a year ago when it was connected to a lemon is still revolving on its first anniversary today.

Mr Anthony Ashill, a clock-maker from Kidderminster, built the lemon-powered motor last year and put it in the window of his shop to entertain children passing by. His invention attracted international attention, and after a year, and with the lemon blackened and shrivelled, the motor is still turning.

"I had the idea that if I put a slit in each end of the lemon and inserted copper at one end and zinc at the other it would act as a battery and power the motor but I had no idea that, electrically speaking, there was so much juice in a lemon," Mr Ashill said.

At 120rpm he has calculated that the lemon has turned the motor round 63,722,800 times.

Cow on motorway

Seven cars were involved in accidents trying to avoid a cow which wandered on to the M1 at Crick, Northamptonshire, yesterday. Another car hit the cow and killed it. Eight people were slightly hurt.

Pots of luck for a few brace of feathered pets

East Grinstead

Wingshaven, a bird sanctuary at Sheffield Park, near Uckfield, East Sussex, has become a refuge for pet poultry saved from Christmas dinner tables.

The birds were bought to fatten up, but they became so tame that the owners could not wring their necks, Mr Donald Harrison, the sanctuary's warden, said yesterday.

He had in care 20 turkeys, chickens and geese. "Some wives do not like telling their husbands what they have done ", he said. "I give them a bunch of feathers to take back as 'proof' that the bird has been killed. Then they serve shop-bought poultry as a substitute."

Severed ear is sewn back on

A man who had his right ear bitten off by two attackers after leaving a public house in Dingle, near the centre of Liverpool, had an emergency operation at the city's Whiston Hospital to have it sewn back on.

The man, who has not been named, was also bitten on the head and arms in the attack, which the police said seemed motiveless.

Dog rescues boy who fell into reservoir

Nottingham

Mr Ronald Muers took a desperate chance when his step-son, aged seven, fell from a jetty into 30ft of freezing water in the reservoir at Sutton in Ashfield, Nottinghamshire.

Mr Muers shouted to Troy, his eight-month dog: "Find", the word he uses when he wants him to retrieve pieces of wood from the lake.

Troy, a German bred Rottweiler, raced off, and plunged in and swam 25 yards to where Allan Martin was struggling and screaming. The dog returned to the shore with Allan clinging to his collar.

"Troy certainly saved Allan's life ", Mr Muers, a miner, said. "The lad was wearing wellingtons, two jumpers, a cardigan and a heavy coat. In another few seconds he would have sunk like a stone.

"I was 150 yards away, too far to do anything, when I saw him fall from the jetty. Troy was our only chance and he did not hesitate."

Postal delay

More than 500 letters posted 10 years ago will be delivered today. Mrs Ellen Maunder found the letters, cards and empty mail bags hidden in the attic of her council house in Oak Ridge, Sketty Park, Swansea.

The man who risked his neck to save Foot

Yet another reason why Europe is so fruitful for photographers is the profusion of fun cemeteries. Taken together with a long and vicious history of religious bigotry, you get gems like this. In a Dutch graveyard two burghers, separated in life by divergent views on the right way to worship the Almighty, are allowed to link hands, although in stony silence. The strict condition is that the detente should take place only after death and across the brick cordon sanitaire which here divides Dutch Reformed from Catholic, even post-mortem.

Woman in coma gives birth to healthy baby

Tel Aviv, Sept 8

A woman in a come for over four months after a road accident gave birth to ta healthy 5lb boy at the weekend.

The obstetrician who delivered the baby by Caesarian section at the Sapir medical centre in Kfar Saba said the case appeared to be the first of its kind in medical history where both mother and child survived.

The baby was kept in an incubator for 24 hours after birth. The 34-year-old mother who has two other children, is still unconscious and is being kept alive as before by heart and resparotiry monitoring and other devices.

Nose sewn back

Surgeons have sewn back the nose of Nicholas Chowms, aged 2, of Cromer, Norfolk, which was severed when he fell through the glass front door of his home. His condition in the Norfolk and Norwich Hospital yesterday was reported to be comfortable.

Trains held up by live wire tramp

Exeter

A super-tramp's ingenuity halted all trains on the Penzance to Paddington main line and brought a bomb disposal squad into action.

In his den in the arch of a railway viaduct the tramp had rigged up electric light, heaters and a small cooker ready for a hard winter.

He had tapped the cable supplying street lights alongside the viaduct at Camel's Head, Plymouth. Connexions were made safe with junction-boxes sealed with tape.

But he made one mistake: he ran the wires across the railway sleepers. A sharp-eyed British Rail technician spotted them.

The area was sealed off while a Navy bomb squad investigated. After 90 minutes the alert was called off. The disposal team traced the wires to the tramp's den, but he was not in residence.

"Perhaps he has gone down to our showrooms to report a power failure", an electricity board engineer, suggested.

Boy sacrificed

Kuala Lumpur — A 16-year-old boy was beheaded and offered as a human sacrifice by a Chinese medium seeking the lucky number for a weekly lottery, the *New Straits Times* reported. The medium and three other men were arrested.

TWINS REACH 100

Identical twin sisters Naimi Bomanson and Elin Hagmark made statistical history yesterday when they celebrated their joint 100th birthday in Mariehamn on Finland's Aaland Islands. Stastisticians said there was a one in 700 million chance of such an event. —

Cat wins pools

Aarhus, Dec 2—With the help of his cat, a 23-year-old Danish shipping clerk has won the jackpot of 950,000 kroner (£68,000) in the state-run football pool.

Mr Jan Trane got his cat Dixie to move a dice cup to decide the results of English football matches.

Promises . . .

Foix — A woman of 22 was fined 2,000 francs (about £180) for stripping at a local dance when the band leader promised to reward her with a free television set and tape recorder. He did not keep the promise.

Undertakers missed

Kuala Lumpur, Jan 26.—A wave of deaths from drinking Samsu, a home-made brew, has caused a problem at Kulim, 180 miles north of here. Among the 29 moonshine victims were all but one of the local undertakers.

Sleep slimmer

Nice — A woman weighing 136 lb (about 10 stones) lost 19 lb 4 oz after being in a medically controlled hypnotic slimming sleep for a world record of 300 hours, doctors announced here yesterday.

35 electrocuted

Delhi — Thirty-five passengers were electrocuted when an overcrowded intercity bus carrying old bicycles on its roof came in contact with roadside electricity wires, the Uttar Pradesh state police said.

Marathon on nails

Mr Kenneth Owen, Baptist minister at Mount Pleasant Church, Barry, South Glamorgan, yesterday broke his earlier record of 81 hours 8½ minutes for resting on a bed of nails for YMCA charities.

Why the Pill's success rate is low in Asia

Colombo — Men who wore condoms on a finger or took the Pill meant for their wives were two reasons for contraceptives often being ineffective in Asia, a United Nations report said yesterday.

The report to the Third Asian and Pacific Population Conference related that remote Asian villagers had been shown how to wear condoms in demonstrations with a bamboo pole. When field workers returned several months later they were confronted by groups of irate pregnant women. Inquiries disclosed that men had been wearing condoms on a finger or keeping them on a bamboo pole.

Investigators also discovered that in many instances condoms had been boiled or swallowed. The most common pitfall with the Pill, the report said, was that men were taking it instead of women.

Unwary wife

Bonn — Housewife Elisabeth Gscheidle stuck a 90 pfennig stamp on a postcard unaware that it was a rare collector's item worth 20,000 marks (£5,200), the *Bild Zeitung* reported yesterday. Frau Gscheidle should have known better because her husband was Minister of Posts in the Schmidt Government and had carefully put aside the stamp.

Soup was made of man's hands

Tokyo, Sept 25.—At least 50 people unsuspectingly ate the hands of a murdered gang leader that had been cooked in a soup and served at a Chinese street stall here on July 5, police said today.

Shoichi Murakami was killed with kitchen knives by five men and his body cut into small pieces to avoid identification, they said. The hands were put in the soup to get rid of fingerprints. Five people have been arrested.

Dungeon ordeal

Mrs Debbie Reynolds, mother of two, from Hambledon, Surrey, spent Sunday night alone in the ghostly London Dungeon, near London Bridge, to raise £3,000 for the Royal National Life-boat Institution.

Dogs attack mail vans

Tyre-biting by packs of dogs has reached such proportions in the Western Isles that the Post Office is considering suspending deliveries by mail vans in some areas.

Trying to get out

Walter Hudson, a six-foot American Indian, used to have a problem. "For breakfast," he explains, "I'd eat two pounds of bacon, a dozen eggs, a dozen rolls, jam and coffee. Then about noon I'd send out for four Big Macs, four double cheeseburgers, eight boxes of fries, six little pies and six quarts of soda. For supper I'd have maybe three ham steaks, about six baked sweet potatoes, six or seven baked white potatoes, butter, stuffing, the works. Then after that there'd be snacks — potato chips, cupcakes and sometimes ice cream."

Walter weighed 40 stone, and tended to stay at home reading the Bible and waiting for the next truckload of food. In fact, he did not leave the house for 18 years. Eventually, after he got stuck in his bedroom doorway and had to be cut free by carpenters, he went on a diet and lost 30 stone. But now, even though Walter is slim and trim, he has discovered that he still can't get out and about. He is agoraphobic.

Visions find an 'Agatha Christie' murderer

Washington, Dec 16

A particularly gruesome murder has been uncovered in North Carolina, in circumstances very similar to Agatha Christie's last novel, *Sleeping Murder*. In the book, a woman returns to her childhood home, where events trigger memories long-suppressed of the time when she saw the murdered body of her mother.

In the North Carolina case, Mrs Annie Perry recently started having "visions" of the time her father disappeared in April, 1944. She was then 10. She told the police last week that "on Easter morning she saw her mother in the kitchen and the sink full of pots and pans of bloody water".

Later that day she saw her father's body almost naked in an unused room. During the night she heard "butchering sounds".

The family lived on a farm, and had an outside privy. In the following week, when using the privy she looked down the hole and saw her father's face floating.

Her mother, Mrs Winnie Cameron, reported her husband missing and in due course obtained a divorce, on grounds of desertion.

When the daughter recently began to have "visions" she went to a psychiatrist who sent her to the police.

They took the matter seriously enough to obtain a search warrant. She took them to the site of the privy, where they dug and found human bones.

On Friday afternoon the police found Mrs Cameron. She had shot herself, leaving a suicide note in which she confessed to the murder of her husband.

WOMAN TO BE HER MOTHER'S STEPMOTHER

A 20-year-old woman will become stepmother to her mother when she marries her step-grandfather in Johannesburg today.

Susanna Van Zul is to marry Mr Silas Van Aswegen, 62, the widower of Susanna's grandmother, who was a widow herself with a daughter—Susanna's mother—when she married Silas. Susanna fell in love with "grandad" after her grandmother died.

Wife's arm cut off

Nairobi, Dec. 13—Lawrence Kareko, a Kenyan farmer, was jailed for six months today after admitting he chopped off his wife's arm with a machete. "It was due to the pain and annoyance of finding my wife committing adultery", he told the court. "I am very repentant".

Brain survivor

Peking.—A man aged 31, has survived for 15 years with only half his brain after an operation, the New China news agency said. He could do simple work in a factory with only his left cerebral hemisphere. He was described as coureous and happy and had suffered no damage in understanding, memory or surroundings.

CAKES POISON 600

Six hundred schoolchildren and several adults went down with food-poisoning in north-west Portugal after eating cakes at a tea party commemorating the International Year of the Child.

Youth impaled

Mr Stephen Price, aged 17 of Walsall, who impaled himself on a bar after falling from a bridge, was found after tapping out an SOS message on a rail. His condition in hospital yesterday was "fairly comfortable".

Chickens die in fire

Seven thousand chickens died yesterday when fire swept through a breeder unit at Imperial Foods poultry farm at Bilsthorpe, near Newark, Nottinghamshire.

SWAN SONG

Two trumpeter swans at the Wildfowl Trust in Slimbridge, Glos., have confounded experts by producing four cygnets, at the age of 28. The swans, presented to the Queen by the Canadian Government in 1952, normally stop producing when they are about 15.

FINGER METHOD TO PULL TEETH

A Chinese dentist has extracted more than 30,000 teeth by finger pressing at several acupuncture points without the use of drugs or anesthesia, the Hsinhua news agency reported yesterday.

Dr Kung Hsueh-pin said patients feel only slight pain, lose less blood, and 97 per cent. of the extractions caused no damage to the surrounding tissue and no other side effects."

A RARE BIRDIE

A Seagull dropped a stunned mullet on a Queensland golfer playing in the Sunshine Coast Open golf championship in Melbourne. Mr Noël Staatz was on the 15th green and fancied to win when the mullet, weighing about 1·5lb, was dropped from about 300ft. He was knocked down.

Junket for robbers was police trap

New York, March 17

The hand-drawn sign in the front window of the charabanc read: "Good Buy Charter". It should have been spelt differently, for the coach party of 25, who had been expecting a jolly day's gambling and drinking at the casinos in Atlantic City, were instead driven to prison.

It was the culmination of another of those police under cover operations which cause such merriment when they are disclosed here. Good Buy was the name the police gave to a shop they established five months ago in Manhattan's Diamond District, on West 47th Street off Fifth Avenue, for the purpose of buying stolen property.

During that time, police say they bought goods worth $2.5m (£1.1m) although they paid only $8,000 for them. The discrepancy was caused by the fact that much of the property was stolen bonds which are hard to sell and therefore command a low price on the undercover market.

After they set up the shop, describing themselves as "buyers of gold and silver", police said it was not long before word of their willingess to buy stolen property circulated in the underworld.

They received a steady flow of offers and propositions, including one from a man who wanted their help in killing and robbing a Brooklyn couple.

Soon the operators of Good Buy informed their clients that, to celebrate the imminence of spring, they would be organizing a gambling trip to Atlantic City to reward their loyal patrons. There would be free champagne and $1,000 of stake money each. The day trippers were to meet yesterday morning at Sullivan's Bar on Eighth Avenue at 46th Street, not far from the Diamond District.

When the group of 25 had assembled they were all placed under arrest. Then they were loaded on to the coach and driven, not to the seaside, but to the police station.

There, 11 of the 25 were charged with possessing stolen goods and the remainder held for questioning. Police are still looking for 18 of their customers who, with apparent foresight, did not go.

Daunting span : The 6ft moustache of Mr John Roy, of Braintree, Essex, displayed during a visit to Toronto. It took 41 years to grow.

What sort of person is getting the benefit of higher education at our historic universities nowadays? A circular sent to students by the Tutor for Rooms at Jesus College, Cambridge says: "Gentlemen are reminded that the habit of eating from the floor may well result in damage to carpets, and that such damage is chargeable at the end of the academic year."

Blue jumper

Houston — Using suction cups. a man wearing a mask. blue wig and blue jump suit climed up the side of the 71-storey Allied Bank Plaza building in Houston, put on a parachute, leaped off and landed on the roof of a car park. Police arrested him for trespassing.

Police moved on by prostitutes

Kassel, West Germany, June 25.—Prostitutes won a battle today to stay in a building which they had shared with a police station for five years. The police moved out. after five years of urging the landlord to evict the prostitutes.

Something fishy about tuna

Brussels. — National surveys of wholesalers, supermarkets and fishmongers by the Belgian Consumers' Association discovered that 99 per cent of fish advertised as tuna is really shark.

Unlucky 13th

Bonn — A West German motoring club. warning drivers to take extra care today. said statistics bear out the superstition that Friday the 13th is unlucky. On three such days in 1984, road deaths were 48 per cent above average and crashes increased by 30 per cent.

Foul-smelling tramp who sniffs out debts lands up in court

THE stink of a filthy tramp has brought the sweet smell of success to a debt collection agency. Only twice have firms failed to pay up since the agency began a year ago.

The "tramp" is ANDREW SMULIAN, 20, whose motto is: "Pay up or throw up."

He wears tattered foul-smelling clothes, blackens his face and then sits in debtors' offices until his stench forces the management to give in.

But yesterday he appeared clean, tidy and odourless, at Bow Street magistrates' court charged with insulting behaviour likely to cause a breach of the peace. He pleaded not guilty and was given unconditional bail until the case is heard on Nov. 12.

Andy Smulian yesterday.

Dublin visit

The idea occurred to Mr Peter Stokes, a magazine editor, on a visit to Dublin when an evil-smelling tramp passed him in the street. "Just the sort of person to collect debts," he thought.

So when his magazine, ENTREPRENEUR, was short of a story ie wrote about his idea, and the response was immediate.

"Suddenly we were inundated with people asking us to collect debts for them," said Miss Diane Weller, the magazines advertising director. So Mr Stokes started the service at £30 a time through an associate company, London Manhattan.

"At first to make the smells, we let fish go rotten and sewed it into the lining of the tramp's coat. But this didn't have enough lingering power. Then our tramp, Andy, went back to his school chemistry master who dreamed up this little bottle of stuff," she said.

Trade secret

The ingredients of the smelly substance are a closely-guarded trade secret, but Smulian said yesterday: "The formula? Compost kept in plastic bags and then further treated by a laboratory in Ealing, but it is absolutely non-toxic.

"It is in liquid form and I dilute it as necessary. Full strength and with a following wind you would get me 65 yards down the road."

Miss Weller said: "I've experienced the smell myself and believe me, it's filthy. It's a fruity smell.

Smulian, who lives in Golders Green and says girl friends "come and go," has permanently blocked sinuses—"otherwise I couldn't do the job.

"I love my job. I have worked in other places as a clerk, but never had job satisfaction before.

"Now I enjoy just walking down the street. I don't believe in violence, but I do believe pople should pay debts.

Smulion leaves the magazine's offices in Dallington Street, Islington, in tattered trousers, jumper full of holes, top coat tied with string, army boots which shrow his toes, skin blackened with charcoal and accompanied b ythe most repugnant odour.

At the offices of the debtors he goes into the reception area, sits down and says nothing. Usually the management can't write out a cheque quickly enough.

"Our tramp has never had to wait anywhere for more than half an hour," said Miss Weller. "The staff threaten to leave if the management won't pay.

"The tramp carries a letter which explains that he is acting on behalf of a client and is instructed to wait for a cheque. He never speaks. He has never been assaulted — most people can't bear to touch him."

Asked if, because of the court case, Smulian and other "smellies" would be continuing their activities, Mr Stokes said: "We shall have to think about this and take advice, but it will be a pity if smellies have to be barred because they have been so successful.

"Their art is in getting the two sides—the creditor and the debtor—together. They are, I suppose you could say, a sort of catalyst."

Saved by dolphins

Johannesburg, May 30.—Four fishermen have claimed they were saved from being dashed to death on rocks in a thick fog by a school of dolphins which nudged them into a sheltered cove near Cape Town.

Tug-o'-war tragedy

Harrisburg, Pennsylvania, June 13.—A rope-pulling game at a school here turned into tragedy when the nylon rope snapped, severing the fingers of four of the children and injuring 150, including teachers.

Sect drown eight children 'to appease God'

Rio de Janeiro, May 4.—A fanatical religious sect in northeastern Brazil hurled eight small children into the sea in a mass human sacrifice "to appease God", the police said today.

The children were aged between eight months and five years. Some of the older ones who struggled to the shore were thrown back until they disappeared. The police have arrested 21 people, including the parents of the victims.

The human sacrifice took place on Saturday night in a ceremony on a beach near Salvador, 1,060 miles north of Rio de Janeiro.

Woman kept in cellar for 29 years

Athens, Nov 7

The brother and two elder sisters of a woman found in a half-savage state after being locked up for 29 years in a filthy village basement were charged today with illegal detention and causing grievous bodily harm.

The woman kept prisoner is Miss Eleni Karyotou. She is now 47 and was apparently shut away at the age of 18 because her parents objected that her love affair with a fellow-villager threatened to break the peasant tradition that elder sisters should marry first.

The police, after a tip-off, searched the family house in Kostalexi, north of Athens, and found the woman naked in a dark, dank basement. She was like a trapped animal, obviously deranged, and had been fed through a small opening in a barred window.

She was taken to Lamia hospital and found to be suffering from muscular atrophy of the limbs, anaemia, and photophobia (the dread of light).

Mr Efthymios Karyotis, the woman's brother, and her two sisters, Olympias and Maria, told the police their sister had been put away by their parents, who are now dead, because she had been mentally unbalanced.

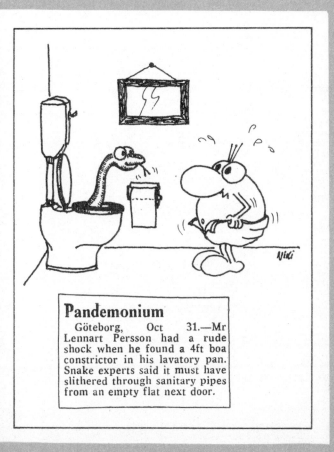

Pandemonium

Göteborg, Oct 31.—Mr Lennart Persson had a rude shock when he found a 4ft boa constrictor in his lavatory pan. Snake experts said it must have slithered through sanitary pipes from an empty flat next door.

Man and wife in head-on crash

Mr Anthony Lions, aged 41, driving a friend's car, was involved in a head-on collision with his own car, which was being driven by his wife, Christina, near their home in Sussex Drive, Walderslade, Chatham, yesterday.

Mr Lion was thrown through the windscreen and both cars were damaged beyond repair. The couple suffered minor injuries.

Vicar resigns after sex change

A middle-aged vicar has resigned from his parish in the diocese of Blackburn, Lancashire, after an operation to turn him into a woman. His former bishop, the Right Rev Robert Martineau, refused last night to make any comment.

The Church of England will not name the vicar, who was unmarried,

Five dismissed over dead mouse

Five women workers at GEC's Xpelair works in Witton, Birmingham, who dropped a dead mouse into an Asian worker's lunchtime curry have been dismissed.

The rest of the workers threatened to walk out unless the five lost their jobs because the mouse almost certainly died from eating rat poison. The Asian was taken to hospital

Blood of saint liquefies

Naples, May 1.—The "miracle of St Januarius"—the liquefaction of what is claimed to be the clotted blood of the fourth century martyr and patron saint of Naples—occurred last night, church officials said.

It liquefied, as it usually does twice a year, after hour-long prayers led by Cardinal Corrado Ursi of Naples.

WAR ON SPITTING

A campaign against spitting has been launched in Peking. Residents spit anywhere including in restaurants and at the theatre.

Parents preserve murdered girl's brain

Oakland, California, Oct 6.— The brain of a murdered 15-year-old girl has been preserved in a frozen state here because her parents hope that it can one day be used to reconstitute a person exactly like her.

"We feel it is a long shot, but it is our way of expressing our belief in life and our rejection of the casual acceptance of murder and death in our society", said Mr Robert Wilson, whose daughter Patricia was murdered on Sunday.

Mr Arthur Quaife, president of Trans-Time, a cryonics (body-preserving) organization, said that at some future time it was hoped scientists would be able to re-create Patricia.

DOG SAVES WOMAN

A dog died saving the life of a woman in southern Yugoslavia when it seized a live electric cable in its jaws and pulled it away from the unconscious woman, the Belgrade, newspaper, *Politika Express*, reported yesterday.

QUICK AND THE DEAD

A police officer was amazed when a hearse shot past him at 70 m p h, with a coffin in the back. Undertaker Robert Raper, of Seamer Road, Scarborough, North Yorkshire yesterday was fined £30 by magistrates at Newark, Notts, for exceeding 50 m p h in a hearse on the Great North Road while taking a body to Scarborough for burial.

'NO LAUGHING' ORDER

When jolly Hannah Buckler, 44, ordered a drink in her local, she was astounded when the barman replied: "Only if you promise not to laugh." She thought he was joking, but he was not.

For Hannah, a tobacco factory worker, of Cox's Drive, Sholing, Southampton, has a deafening chortle.

"I just broke down and cried," she said yesterday. Mr Ernest Lee, landlord at the Cliff Hotel, Woolston, Southampton, would make no comment.

Thomas Crapper fails to win a plaque

A suggestion that a blue plaque should be erected to commemorate a former home of the Victorian sanitary engineer, Thomas Crapper, after earnest consideration has been rejected by the historic buildings committee of the Greater London Council.

The committee decided that "memorable though Crapper's name might be in popular terms," evidence from the Patents Office showed that he was not a notable inventor or pioneer in his field.

Dragon in distress

A WELSH dragon on a flying visit to London for yesterday's England-Wales rugby international first had to appear in court, charged with being drunk and disorderly . . . and claimed wrongful arrest.

The dragon (above), alias Edward Prosser, a 38-year-old interior designer, was alleged to have "leaked" in public. But he told West London magistrates court: "Basically, it was wrongful arrest because I am an animal and not a human. Where are dragons supposed to do their natural things?"

The courtroom burst into laughter as he strolled into the dock in his full red dragon regalia, with wings, a long tail and gold teeth. A police spokesman had said earlier that Prosser would have to appear in his outfit because he had no other clothes with him.

Prosser, who removed his headgear for the brief hearing, pleaded guilty to being drunk and disorderly in Hammersmith on Friday night. He was fined £10, but not before complaining: "I was given the wrong breakfast. I should have had coal and a box of firelighters and they gave me egg on toast."

After the case, Prosser, from Porth, Glamorgan, said: "I don't know why they picked on me. There were 15 of us doing it. I don't think I was too conspicuous."

Scatter my ashes in goal, student wrote

A Notts County supporter wrote to the club saying that he was going to commit suicide and asking that his ashes should be scattered in the goalmouth.

The letter said: "In a few days time this club should be approached by my parents with a request for my ashes to be scattered in the goalmouth at Meadow Lane. This is one of my last wishes before I commit suicide.

"I have been a Notts County supporter for more than nine years and a season ticket holder for the last five seasons. So I feel that this request is fully justified and I would be extremely grateful if the management of the club would grant it."

A club official said: "We have no objection to carrying out this request if asked to do so by the family".

Former slave dies aged 119

Bunnell, Florida — Mr Ike Ward, a woodcutter born a slave on a Virginia plantation on Christmas Day 1862, when Abraham Lincoln was president, has died here aged 119, one day after he entered a nursing home for the first time.

He was married 16 times and outlived all his wives. For the past five years he was looked after by Miss Rachel Hall, a 62-year old cousin. He had worked, ploughing his own one-acre plot, until two weeks ago.

He was always in perfect health, never used a walking stick or wore glasses.

Soft landing

Nantes (AFP) — A two-year-old girl survived a fall from an eighth floor window, when she landed on sheets drying on a line.

Sex once a week enough, appeal judge says

Turning turtle: "Scuttlebutt", a 12lb desert tortoise uses a wheel screwed to his shell to help him go round corners while his broken leg heals. It was installed by the Animal Foundation in Eugene, Oregon, after a car accident.

● This is 78-year-old Alfonsina Cottini, perhaps the oddest of Italy's rapidly growing host of village saints. Signorina Alfonsina, who lives with her sister in the tiny Alpine village of Craveggio, near Lake Maggiore, suddenly retired permanently to bed more than 11 years ago.

Since then, according to her proponents, she has neither drunk nor eaten; nor has she eliminated anything. On the basis of this, Alfonsina—who is said to have reclined beatifically on her back ever since she took to bed—has become a cult figure for busloads of pilgrims from all over the world, and is thought to cause miraculous cures in those who come to her bedside.

Alfonsina is an extraordinary sight stretched out on her small iron bed, surrounded by hundreds of photographs and mementoes left by her visitors. Eyes closed, she breathes heavily and wears a blissful smile.

But not everyone in the village is convinced of her saintliness. Local cynics claim that she rises in the night and raids the fridge—as well as doing other essential things. After complaints about large sums of money changing hands near the old lady's bedside, the church authorities decided that local priests should have nothing to do with the cult. It is just as well: a three-man judicial commission has just reported that Alfonsina does emit discharges "of a remarkable potency."

Late delivery

An airmail letter arrived in Bristol yesterday from Wyoming in the United States. It had been posted in 1948.

Couple's night to remember

Milan, Jan 24.—A naked couple found inside a parked car, who said they were celebrating their wedding anniversary, were arrested here for obscenity, outrage to public morals, threatening law officers, violence and resisting arrest, the police said today.

The couple insulted a policeman who ordered them to dress and drove away at high speed, but police shot the tyres of their car.

Carry on running

Sydney, July 18.—Five prisoners taking part in Cessnock Jail's weekend race kept right on running after they had crossed the finishing line and were still at large today.

Grant for tallest man

Karachi, Sept 1.—President Zia ul-Haq has authorized a monthly grant of 500 rupees (£26) to Pakistan's tallest man, Mr Alam Channa, aged 22, who stands 8ft 2in.

73 IN A MINI

Seventy three scouts and cubs from Leckhampton, Cheltenham, crammed into and on to a mini car yesterday and claimed a world record for the most people in a mini.

Money too hot for thieves

Thieves worked through the night to open a safe, but when they eventually burnt off its side at offices of agricultural engineers in Banbury they found only charred banknotes and cheques.

The owner said the heat from the thieves' cutting equipment set fire to the contents of about £150 in notes and cheques.

Missing girl is found in jungle

Jakarta — A 12-year-old Indonesian girl, believed to have drowned six years ago, has been found living as a jungle creature in a south Sumatran swamp, the official Antara news agency reported.

Hunters found the girl, Imiyati, lying on the marshy ground, her naked body covered with moss. They at first mistook her for an orang-utan ape. She was unable to speak and could only make waving gestures with her hands.

Beaten by moles

Mole hills on two council-owned football pitches in Peterborough have forced two clubs to use other grounds. The council is providing other pitches free of charge until it finds ways of eliminating the mole hills.

Sticking point

Children visiting Sudbury Hall Museum of Childhood in Derbyshire can climb a 20ft mock-up of a Victorian chimney to experience what it was like being a Victorian chimney sweep. But because today's children are plumper than their nineteenth century counterparts, many are getting stuck.

Six-hour chicken chase on M5

About 40 chickens were captured by RSPCA inspectors yesterday after dozens fell off a lorry between Clevedon and the Avon bridge on the M5, near Bristol.

Two inspectors spent six hours rescuing the chickens. The lorry driver continued his journey unaware of the incident.

Angry parent bites off referee's ear

Melbourne

An umpire (referee) in an under 12's Australian Rules football match had part of his left ear bitten off on Sunday as he tried to break up a brawl between parents.

The ear was found trodden into the ground, after the game, some time after the incident, and was packed in ice and rushed to a Melbourne hospital.

But last night Mr Alan Davis's wife Pam said she feared the operation had not been successful."

Mr Davis described how "the cowardly mongrel" had run behind a coach like a dingo after the attack. Parents had come "in droves on to the field, their women kicking and punching everything".

Typewriter ban

Bucharest — A new government decree prohibits the owning or use of typewriters by Romanians who have a criminal record or pose "a danger to public order or state security". Private citizens must tell police of typewriters they own or want to buy.

Head delivered

Jakarta — A severed human head covered with fresh blood was delivered to the newspaper to the newspaper *Suara Indonesia* (Voice of Indonesia) in the city of Malang. The identity of the victim was not known.

Wrong course

Taipei — Police are investigating a pigeon race in which more than 2,000 birds took part but only five returned. The rest apparently ended their lives on the tables of local restaurants, after being trapped in giant hilltop nets along the race route.

For whom . . .

Adligenswil — Mr Vit Stupka, a Czechoslovak, has been refused Swiss citizenship because a village meeting decided his dislike of cow bells showed he was not properly assimilated despite 14 years' residence in Switzerland.

Zoo mauling

New York — A man escorted from Central Park Zoo on Saturday after trying to get into the elephant and lion cages was found dead yesterday in the polar bear cage, apparently mauled to death.

Slip costs £800,000

Mrs Joan White, aged 51, of Kendray, Barnsley, needed medical attention after learning that she and her bedridden husband had not won £800,000 because their winning football pools coupon had been mislaid.

Blaze victim

The charred body of Miss Elizabeth Lucas, aged 84, was found sitting upright in a kitchen chair yesterday in the burnt-out remains of her home in Betchworth, Surrey.

TV for budgie

Bluey the budgerigar got his own three-inch £250 colour television set for Christmas, as a gift from his owner, Mrs Elizabeth Porter, aged 36, of Cumpsty Road, Litherland, Merseyside.

Dead shot

Zurich — A bank robber accidentally shot himself in the thigh and bled to death in the getaway car; his accomplice lost part of the £59,000 loot in seeking help.

Baby number 19 for moor man

The birth of Hazel to Mr John Knight and Claire, who shares his life on Bodmin Moor with Carole, his wife, brings the number of children he has fathered to 19. Mr Knight's wife has borne him ten children and Hazel's mother has borne him nine. She has also had five by her former husband.

Mr Knight is entitled to well over £100 a week in state support for his family.

Rover hammered

A motorist set about his Rover 2000 with a sledgehammer after it broke down yesterday on the M5 near Gloucester. The bodywork of the 14-year-old car, which had just been serviced, was extensively damaged.

Pigs don't fly

St Petersburg, Florida
Plans to parachute three pigs to highlight a "Great American Pig-out" festival were scrapped under pressure from a local animal rights group who said it would have been cruel and inhumane.

Beefburger bravery

Mr Gerry Gardner, a company director who hit a thief with a packet of frozen beefburgers after he took £1,600 from a supermarket at St Neots, Cambridgeshire, forcing him to drop the money, was rewarded yesterday with £100 and an outsize packet of beefburgers.

Mouse rap

New Orleans — A woman who claimed she ordered fried chicken in a fast-food restaurant but got a large batter-fried mouse has filed a lawsuit seeking $225,000 (£145,000) in damages.

Lucky 13

Taipei — Thirteen has proved a lucky number for Hua Ting-kuo. After being sentenced to death 12 times in the past nine years for the murder of his mother, he was finally acquitted here at the end of his thirteenth trial on the basis of new evidence.

200lb catch

Two hundred pounds of river fish, which had apparently got into the cooling towers at Radcliffe-on-Soar power station, near Nottingham, as eggs or fry, were removed when the system was drained for maintenance.

Walls of gold

Perth — Officials at the state mint factory in Perth said about 1,000 ounces of gold had vapourized during 86 years of refining, and the walls and ceiling would have to be smelted to separate the $A500,000 (£243,000) worth of gold from the brickwork. The factory is being relocated.

High notes

Perth — An English entertainer, Peter Maxwell, is claiming a world altitude record for piano playing in a hot-air balloon after going through a medley of old favourites at a height of 5,926 ft.

Young love

Nairobi — Muhammad Aloo, aged 100, married a 14-year-old girl in a Muslim ceremony in north-eastern Kenya. The best man was aged 86.

Bogus police

Surrey police are searching for imposters posing as traffic police who they say have been detaining motorist in Surrey for up to an hour at the roadside and insulting them.

Costly kiss

Bangkok – A trainee nurse handed in a piece of someone's tongue at a police station here. She apparently bit it off a man who forced a kiss upon her.

Solid beer

Kobe — A Japanese company is launching a "solid beer" next Tuesday. Mixed with apple and lemon juice and solidified into a jelly it will be sold in square glasses.

Mummified baby is found in cupboard

The mummified body of a new-born baby has been found in a bedroom cupboard in a house in Wolverhampton, where it had been locked away for at least forty years.

Police said there was no sign of injury to the body, which had been tightly wrapped in clothing and then covered by pages of newspapers and magazines dating from 1915 to 1933.

The find was made on Saturday afternoon at a house in Trysall Road, Wolverhampton, as relatives of the late occupant, a spinster, were sorting through her belongings.

The remains of the child had been hidden in a steel chest in the cupboard.

A police spokesman said: "The body has been examined by a Home Office pathologist, and he is of the opinion that it had remained undiscovered for at least forty years, possibly much longer". He said the child was perfectly formed. The coroner is to be informed.

The spinster and a male lodger who had once lived at the house both died earlier this year.

Leading with his chin: An American apiarist allows bees to swarm on him and form a "beard".

Darker shade of pale

Johannesburg, June 26.—A tramp taken to a whites-only hospital here was ordered to be scrubbed before admission—because he was so dirty no one could tell whether he was white or black. He turned out to be white and was allowed in.

Tattoo clues to body in ditch

A tattooed woman, whose dismembered body was found in Essex yesterday, may have been the victim of a jealous lesbian lover, the police said. The woman, aged about thirty, had the names of women tattooed on her arms and hands.

A taxi driver walking his dog at High Beach, Loughton, found the body which was in three dustbin liner sacks in a ditch.

Severed fingers sewn back

Nice, Sept 1.—Two fingers severed from the hand of a girl of two were sewn back in place in a series of micro-surgery operations today at a Nice hospital.

The girl, Faissa Mesbhahi, had her fingers cut off by an escalator here. Firemen dismantled the escalator and recovered the fingers.

280 bacon pigs die

More than 280 bacon pigs died in a fire at a barn on Beckfield Farm, Sandon, near Stevenage, Hertfordshire, yesterday. The damage was estimated at £45,000.

Ferry food wins Ronay foul fodder award

Tear gas attack

Karachi, March 17.—Scores of patients left hospital beds in Karachi to escape tear gas fired by the police at medical students demonstrating outside, student leaders said today.

Hot gospel

Grand Rapids, Michigan. — The Rev Dwight Wymer has agreed to stop giving electric shocks to young people at his bible class "so they can hear the word of God". The local prosecutor said although the use of a six-volt battery was not illegal, it could be a potetial health hazard.

Sisters are reunited

Two elderly sisters have been reunited 41 years after being separated during the London blitz. They were in the same ward at an Exeter hospital awaiting operations for the same complaint. Mrs Gladys McKenzie, aged 71, and Mrs Queenie King, aged 74, were near neighbours for 13 years in Paignton, Devon, without realizing it.

He's very attached to his phone

IT WAS a sticky situation the night Geoffrey Slaven, of Falconwood Parade, Welling, Kent, became so attached to his phone he had to call the fire brigade.

It happened when his cat knocked over and damaged the phone. Mr Slaven was repairing it when his two dogs knocked over the superglue.

When he picked up the phone he became firmly stuck to it. To call for help he had to dial the ambulance station with a pen between his teeth.

The ambulancemen couldn't help and called the firemen, who called the police. In the end, the firemen cut the cable and took Mr Slaven to hospital where a solvent freed him.

Open and shut case

Paris. — An unlucky French robber stole the contents of a cashier's till at a bank near Paris and then got stuck between the bank's double doors. He fired several shots at the doors but failed to open them.

Eye test 'failure'

A woman motorist aged 83 failed an eye test a few minutes after she had knoced down a woman aged 93 an inquest at Bournemouth heard yesterday. But took another test the next day and passed.

Two-headed terrapin

A two-headed terrapin has been delivered to a pet shop in Westdale Lane, Carlton, Nottinghamshire. "Each head eats separately and sleeps separately", Mr Peter Godfrey, the owner, said.

Teacher's tantrum

Jakarta, March 22.—A teacher in Sumatra, enraged by complaints from his pupils that they did not understand his mathematics lesson, beat two children unconscious and injured 13 others, according to a Jakarta newspaper.

Grant sought for sweeping

Mr Raymond Richards, aged 23, who has been given a £500 Arts Council grant to sweep up rubbish into artistic shapes, said yesterday that he was applying for another £300 to put on a Christmas show.

Mr. Richards of West Bridgford, Nottinghamshire, plans to do his sweeping around the Christmas tree in the centre of the city.

Why small toads affect a deep croak

Male toads have found a clever way of deceiving the females they are courting about their size. The female prefers to mate with big males and, because she normally chooses her partner in the dark, she judges his size by the depth of voice; the larger the toad the deeper the croak.

The potential for deception arises because body temperature also affects the pitch of the croak; a cold toad can give a deeper croak.

An American researcher has now shown that toads seek out the coldest part of the pond to make their croaks deeper. A female who thinks she is mating with a large, warm toad may have been deceived by a small, cold one.

Antelope gores nurse to death

East London, South Africa — A nurse bent over a prostrate antelope, preparing to administer a sedative, when the animal suddenly raised its head and pierced the nurse's throat with a horn.

Woman cleared over mouse in python's tank

A claim that a live, tame mouse was in a state of terror after it was dropped into a python's glass tank as food, was made to Bradford magistrates yesterday.

Experts disagreed and the magistrates, who were told of cases where mice had bitten snakes, dismissed an allegation against a pet shop owner of cruelly terrifying the mouse. They awarded £300 costs against the RSPCA

Aerial greetings case

Mr Bryan Bateson, a flying instructor, of Wrea Green, near Blackpool, is being prosecuted by the Department of Trade for allegedly towing an 80ft birthday greeting to his wife behind his aircraft.

Paris schoolboy routs burglars

—Paris, Feb 23.—French newspapers today paid tribute to a 12-year-old boy who fought off four burglars with an airgun and a penknife.

Nicolas Mataresse was alone at home in the Paris suburb of Franconville when the gang burst in. He shot one in the arm, stabbed another in the shoulder and sent all four running.

Cows derail train

One coach of a passenger train was derailed at Mouldsworth, near Chester, after colliding with a herd of heifers last night. No one was seriously injured.

HOLE SWALLOWS HOUSE AND CAR

Winter Park, Florida, May 10. —A giant hole in the ground slowly expanded and filled with water today after a house had fallen into it with six cars and part of several buildings and a swimmnig pool yesterday. No one was hurt.

Officials estimated the hole, which opened suddenly on Friday night was more than 1,000 ft across and 170 ft deep.—

Jesus claimants' testimony fails

Twenty people claiming to be Jesus Christ have asked for £30,000 left by Mr Ernest Digweed, of Samuel Road, Portsmouth, who was found dead four years ago in a tent in his sitting room. He said in his will that the money was for the Son of God to use at the second coming.

The Public Trustee Office, which is handling the will, said none of the claimants had produced the necessary identification.

The swimming cats of Lake Van are among the little-known curiosities of Turkey's interior.

Belgian gang led by boy of eight

Liège, Dec 29.—Police have arrested a gang of seven boys aged eight to 15 who stole about 90,000 francs (about £1,385) worth of toys and clothes.

The gang leader, aged eight, was parading through the town wearing a 27,000 francs fur coat and carrying two guns. Police said he was terrorizing his mates and forcing them to steal.

Safe route for frogs

Luxembourg, Jan 31.—A specially-designed tunnel for frogs and hedgehogs is to be built under one of the principal country roads of Luxembourg after protests about the slaughter of wildlife by speeding cars.

Woman kept in filthy cellar for 37 years

From Our Own Correspondent
Rome, May 15

Signora Giovanna Lucia Tiana, aged 73, has been brought out of a cellar in the Sardinian village of Bultei, near Sassari, in which she had spent the last 37 years of her life without light, amid rats and filth.

Carabinieri who released her during the weekend were reported as saying that when they found her, the scene was such that they would never want to see its like again.

The woman had been imprisoned in the cellar by her two brothers and sister because they said she was possessed by the devil. All three were arrested.

Sleeper run over

POLICE are seeking a motorist who ran over a French priest asleep in a sleeping bag at the side of a country lane near Bath on Friday night. The priest, from Aix-en-Provence, is in hospital with broken bones.

Couple, police sight UFO

A worker at Heathrow airport told yesterday how he saw an unidentified flying object on the way to the cinema, near Uxbridge, Middlesex. Mr Michael Farmer, aged 34, said he was driving from Hayes to Uxbridge with his wife, when she pointed to a strange light in the sky.

He said: "It was globular, really bright and at first we thought it was some kind of shooting star. It travelled a phenomenal distance in a matter of seconds and all of a sudden stopped. The light went out and we just looked at each other wondering what on earth it could be."

Two police crews near Chertsey spotted a similar object and Addlestone police said last night the object had been sighted by at least 10 officers.

Canine corner : An Arts Council exhibition now at the Institute of Contemporary Arts, in London, includes a selection of paintings meant to appeal to dogs.

Ex-SLAVE, 137, DIES

Charles Smith, a former slave, who said he was 137-years-old, died in a convalescent centre in Barton, Florida, yesterday. He came from Liberia in 1854 and was sold into slavery in New Orleans. He was freed in 1863.

10 widows at funeral

Nairobi, Nov 14.—The 10 widows and 21 children of one of Kenya's oldest men, Kamatui Lomgit, reputed to be well over 100, attended his funeral at Narok, 70 miles west of Nairobi. He had 120 grandchildren.

Firemen cut boy free

Five firemen took 45 minutes to free Christopher Wain, aged two, who was brought to the station in Crownhill, Plymouth, with a cake tin jammed under his chin like a collar. "We tried bolt cutters but had to resort to a hacksaw," a fire officer said.

KILLER HANGED

A man who killed 70 people with a hammer over two years has been hanged in Jaipur, India. Police said Kanpatimar Shankariya, 27, told them he killed because he enjoyed it.—

Cabaret boa strangles performer

La Tuque, Quebec, Aug 21.— An entertainer calling himself Le Grand Melvin and dressed as a vampire was strangled by one of his snakes, a 7ft 6in boa constrictor, during a cabaret performance yesterday.

The club manager said that Melvin, whose real name was Jean-Guy Leclaire, "seemed to miss a reflex and the boa wrapped around his neck" near the end of his first act of the night in the club at La Tuque, about 100 miles north of Montreal.

When the manager noticed Leclaire becoming blue in the face, he called the police, who arrived within minutes. As four policemen struggled to free the entertainer, the manager cut off the snake's head.

"It wasn't a pleasant thing to have to do", he said. "But I had little choice. Unfortunately, Le Grand Melvin was already dead.

DIGGERS FIND 29 BODIES AT MURDER HOUSE

Grisly excavation work will be resumed today at the Chicago home of John Wayne Gacy, who has confessed to police that he killed 32 young men after he had sexual relations with them.

When digging was suspended for the New Year holiday, sheriff's deputies had recovered 29 bodies — the largest number traced to a single person in the history of crime in America, of these, 26 were found beneath Gacy's suburban house.

Gacy is being held in a prison hospital, strapped to his bed "to keep him from hurting himself or others," according to a prison spokesman. He is said to have told police besides the bodies buried under his house, he threw five victims into the Des Plaines River.

BEGGAR'S £11,600

David Manaseh Solomon, who had spent 15 years begging on Singapore's streets, left £11,620.

WIFE No. 23 FOR 'MOST MARRIED MAN'

Glynn Wolfe, of Blythe, California, listed in the "Guiness Book of World Records" as the most married man, increased his score on Monday by taking wife No. 23. Wolfe, who gave his age as 71 and said he had 40 children, exchanged vows with Maria Chavez Wolfe, 21, in Las Vegas.

Wolfe, a former minister, announced last month that he had married Miss Chavez in Blythe in a ceremony he performed himself because the local minister refused, calling him "a sinner."

WHY 'PUP' FAILED TO BARK

An Italian cattle breeder who who bought a strange-looking "puppy" at a fair near Brescia, nothern Italy, wondered why it never barked. At four months old it was strong enough to break a heavy leather leash and when its owner tried to put on another it bit him.

Both master and "dog" were taken to the Brescia hospital, where a veterinary surgeon quickly solved the mystery. "This is no dog. It's a lion cub," he said.

CHICKEN BARBECUE

A lorry loaded with dressed chickens and another carrying barbecue sauce collided on New York's George Washington Bridge yesterday and burst into flames.

HEARTBREAK HIPPO DIES FOR LOVE

A 30-YEAR-OLD hippopotamus whose mate died last year has been destroyed at Copenhagen Zoo because he was pining away.

Rasmus was the third husband of Maren, who was believed to be the world's oldest hippo. When she died from old age at 54, he immediately went into mourning.

"Rasmus, who normally ate up to 60lb of hay, grass, vegetables and bread every day, lost his appetite the day Maren died," said Mr Jens Elmer, a veteran keeper.

Rasmus lost more than 800lb in weight. He refused to eat for days, and his friendliness to keepers turned to hostility.

ATTACK BY SNAKE

Mrs Dulcie Baldwin, 78, woke up in hospital in Sydney where she was recovering from a heart attack and found a deadly tiger snake with its fangs deep in her left hand. A doctor killed it with a length of rubber hose. Mrs Baldwin was seriously ill last night.

CAT ROUND-UP

More than 150 cats living in the British Steel works at Bilston, West Midlands, which closed last month, are to be rounded up by the Albrighton Animal Rescue Team. The corporation will pay veterinary and food bills until the cats are found homes.

GIRL, 10, HAS TWINS

A 10-year-old girl has given birth to twins at the Indiana University Medical Centre. A spokesman said the babies were born six weeks prematurely last week, and weighed 3lb 6oz each. They are staying in hospital while they gain weight.

SUICIDE FOREST

The bodies of 43 people who committed suicide have been recovered this year from Japan's "Forest of no Return," at the foot of Mount Fuji. At least 176 bodies have been recovered since 1975. In 1960, a novel glamorised the forest as a place for peaceful death.

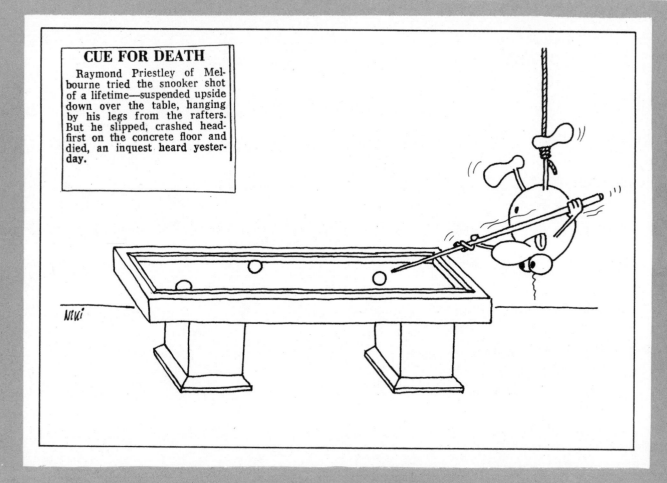

CUE FOR DEATH

Raymond Priestley of Melbourne tried the snooker shot of a lifetime—suspended upside down over the table, hanging by his legs from the rafters. But he slipped, crashed head-first on the concrete floor and died, an inquest heard yesterday.

Mission nuns care for real life 'jungle boy' in India

Delhi, April 19

It appears that the Sisters of Charity, the Catholic missionary order of Mother Teresa of Calcutta, have got on their hands a real life "Mowgli", a boy who goes on all fours because he was brought up among wild animals of northern India, just like Kipling's famous creation in *The Jungle Book*.

The fascination with the idea of feral children is unending but certainly the five sisters at the order's Lucknow house have for the past fortnight been looking after a strange newcomer among their usual run of human destitutes.

"We don't know the real story; we are caring for him but we'd like to show him to doctors or anthropologists", Sister Antonia, the Indian sister in charge, told me in a telephone interview. "He certainly does not talk like a human being but only makes mewing sounds to show when he is pleased."

The boy had been brought from the jungle on Easter Day, Sister Antonia went on, and that was why the mission's priest had recommended them to call him Pascal.

Sister Antonia was cautious when asked if the boy had really been brought up, like Kipling's Mowgli, by animals. The mission priest had not been certain, she added, for the villagers who brought Pascal had also talked about his having been kept in a cage for a year by those who lived near the jungle.

But the sisters had to accustom the boy to eating food normally, having been told that in the wild he had gone round stealing chickens, eating the meat raw and the jungle people had beaten him for this.

Arm sewn back

Johannesburg, Feb 14.—Mr Colin Mason, a British migrant whose left arm was torn off in a Cape Town factory accident, has had it sown back. Surgeons said it would be several months before it would be known if the arm could function again.

RECORD CLIMB BY 'SPIDERMAN'

Chicago, May 25.—Daniel Goodwin, dressed as the comic-book hero Spiderman, today became the first person to climb the world's tallest building—the 110-storey Sears Tower.

Mr Goodwin, aged 25, of Las Vegas, carrying an American flag, used a rope and suction cups to help him climb the 1,454ft building. He was arrested for criminal trespass and disorderly conduct when he reached the roof.

SKELETON FOUND ON CRETE ALTAR

A human sacrificial altar more than 3,600 years old, the first of its kind to be found in Greece, has been discovered in Crete, Ioannis Sakelarakis, an archaeologist, said yesterday in Herakleion, Crete.

On the altar in the western room of a three-chambered Mioan-style temple was found a human skeleton with a bronze sword in the chest. Two other skeletons were found nearby in attitudes clearly indicating a religious ceremony.

RHINO TAKES OVER

A rhinoceros at the Gloucestershire Wildlife Park has adopted a week-old antelope after refusing to mate with her own species. The 14-year-old rhinoceros, Ukhkho, allows the antelope's mother to feed her but frightens away other animals.

ANGLERS' VICTIMS

A swan a day is being saved by Mr Len Baker and his wife from Sparham, Norfolk. Mr Baker urged anglers on the Norfolk Broads not be leave their lines unattended because swans could not see them. In three years the Bakers have rescued more than 400 swans.

Easy as blinking

Berlin.—East Germany has developed security glasses for train drivers. The spectacles have an electronic device emitting a beam that is regularly broken by blinking. If a train driver falls asleep and stops blinking, the train automatically halts.

Jail sackings

Madrid — The head and deputy head of Spain's main top-security jail were dismissed yesterday after the weekend escape of three prisoners who used mock pistols made from soap to overpower guards and steal their uniforms.

Washington's exotic sets of false teeth

Los Angeles, March 21.— George Washington had dentures made from elephants' tusks and lead and the teeth of humans, cows, hippopotami and probably a walrus, but not from wood, a dentist said today.

Dr Reidar Sognnaes, of the University of California here, said that research he had carried out on the first American President produced no evidence that Washington had wooden stumps as teeth, as some people had believed.

Dr Sognnaes, who reported on his findings to a conference of the American Association for Dental Research, said Washington may not have smiled much in portraits, but he had four sets of false teeth.

Studies of parts of the sets, Dr Sognnaes said, showed that some of the teeth were made from the ivory of elephant tusks. Others came from the teeth of hippopotami and were cut into segments and mounted on ivory.

Washington also had teeth from humans, cows and what appeared to be a walrus, Dr Sognnaes added.

Some of Washington's teeth were also made of lead. They were dark and may have looked like wooden stumps, Dr Sognnaes said.

Although ivory is white, it could be stained with coffee, tea and the port wine that Washington was known to like, he added.

He said Washington had two of his own teeth when he became President in 1789 and one was mounted on a denture. Washington also had other human teeth mounted.

A dog's death

New York, Aug 18.—A girl aged 16 walking her dog with a metal lead was seriously injured and the dog died of electric shock when it urinated on a faulty electric sign.

PENALTY $100
DOGS
MUST NOT FOUL
THE FOOTPATH

Matters Arising

How to collect debts

THE reference in our last issue to the diplomacy that sometimes has to be exercised to get an outstanding account settled has brought us a very amusing letter from a reader living in the Loire Valley, Mr. J. P. B. Ross.

He recalls a story, dating from the days of the British Raj, of a trading firm in Bombay that hired a young and inexperienced Indian clerk who claimed to be an expert in written English. As a test his employers gave him their "bad debts" book and invited him to write to some of the less ancient debtors to see if a fresh approach would achieve anything.

The response in the way of cheques, banknotes and bills of exchange was so voluminous that the amazed managing director asked to see what the new recruit had written. The successful letter was in these terms:

Honoured Sir (s)

We have the unprecedented effrontery to draw your attention to the fact that Your Excellenc(y) (ies) have been in debt to our miserable selves in the sum of Rupees .... from the .... to the present time.

If Your Excellenc(y) (ies) cannot find it convenient immediately to take steps to annul this debt, we, your unworthy creditors, will be most reluctantly obliged to take steps that will cause you the utmost astonishment.

Believe, Honoured Sir(s) in the sincerity of this, our expression.

(Signed)......................

Perhaps we ought to consider rewording our own final-demand letter on these lines.

On death row: Rocky, a pit bull terrier, awaits execution at Seattle for his part in a robbery, for which his master was convicted. The dog is vicious.

A mile-long canal goes down the drain

A MARKET town woke today to find that a mile and a half long canal had vanished overnight—down the drain.

It happened when a waterways dredging team was clearing a stretch of the Chesterfield canal at Retford, Nottinghamshire.

The workmen pulled up a heavy iron chain along with cycles, prams and other rubbish.

They yanked the chain . . . and up came a giant plug. Then as astonished workmen watched, the canal gurgled down the plughole and into the nearby River Idle.

It left a family of Danish holidaymakers, who had hired a pleasure boat for a cruising holiday marooned.

A spokesman at Retford said : "The dredging team was clearing out part of the canal near the town when they pulled up this huge chain. Apparently they did not realise what it was because they dragged it up to find a plug on the end. This allowed all the water to drain into the nearby river.

"The canal is used by pleasure boats because it passes through some attractive countryside. We understand that having fitted a new plug it will take at least a week to refill—and that will not solve the problem of the Danish holidaymakers who have somehow got to get their boat back by this weekend."

● Discovery of the plug—probably in existence since 1777 when the canal was constructed—has solved one riddle. There has been a leakage for years "and now we know where the water has been going," said the Waterways Authority.

DOWN THE DRAIN—canal worker Bill Thorpe with the plug that emptied a mile-and-a-half of canal at Retford, Nottinghamshire, today.

China's hairy people

YU ZHENYUAN is 14 months old and except for the palms of his hands and the soles of his feet, he is covered in hair. His birth in Liaoning, China in 1978 was a sensation but his parents, a young peasant couple, soon discovered they were not alone.

Yu's birth led to the discovery of 32 hair covered people in ten Chinese provinces. In the West,

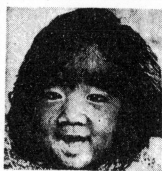

the condition—congenital hypertrichosis lanuginosa universalis —is so rare that experts know it only through medical text books and fairground histories of "ape men" and "wolf women" in sideshows and circuses. The cause of the mutation is unknown but the Chinese sufferers are described as of normal intelligence, although many, not surprisingly, have psychological problems.

Surgeons sew on severed hand

Surgeons at Withington Hospital, Manchester, have stitched back a man's severed hand in an eight-hour operation. Mr Roger Hampson, aged 32, is the first man to have a complete hand sown on using a new microscopic technique.

Mr Hampson was operating a circular bench saw at his woodwork supplies shop in Didsbury, when the accident occurred.

A VINTAGE NAME TO CONJURE WITH

After along battle Mr Peter Dodgson, a Worcestershire businessman, will be marketing his home produced wine as Chateau Piddle.

Mr Dodgson wants to use the name in honour of his village, North Piddle. He points out that French wines are named after the area where they are produced.

He was refused permission to register his wine as Piddle because he was told it was not an accurate description of the contents of the bottle. But now he has been informed that although he will not be allowed an official entry in the register of trade names he can market the product under the name of his choice.

Nudes only

Houston, Texas
Residents of an apartment complex here must choose between their clothes and their homes by March 1. The landlord has told them that the complex will have areas in which Nudity is mandatory, including the swimming pool, sauna and whirlpool.

Witch hunt

Zebediela, South Africa – A man and woman thought by fellow villagers to be witches were tethered to the rear of a lorry and burnt alive over the weekend. Their deaths brought to 12 the number of people burnt as witches in three months.

Airline finds dentures

Pan American officials at Heathrow believe they have found the dentures belonging to Mr Venkat Ali, the passenger from Pakistan who recently reported that the teeth had disappeared while he was asleep at the airport. A passenger had handed in a set, but now Mr Ali cannot be traced.

Nose sewn back

A veterinary surgeon near Taunton, Somerset, has sewn back the nose of a lurcher dog which was ripped off by a fox during a savage fight in which the fox was killed. It will not be known for a few days whether the operation was a success.

GROOM SAYS 'NO' TWICE

Herr Heinz Kommer, 35, is Austria's candidate for most reluctant bridegroom of the year. Twice in one day he took his West German bride, Fräulein Christa Denecke, 30, to the register office in Graz, but both times when asked "do you take this woman . . .? he answered firmly "No."

"It was human error on my part," said Herr Kommer "Maybe I'll try again in October after the summer holidays."

Burglar brought the house down

Anthony Brown broke into a house to steal copper piping and blew it up. He had removed the piping from a live gas supply and then lit a match so that he could see in the dark, Southwark Crown Court was told yesterday.

Brown, aged 42, of no fixed address, survived the explosion unhurt and carried on stripping the central heating system as flames surrounded him.

He returned to the destroyed house, in Fulham, south-west London, the next day to steal more and was caught by the police investigating the explosion.

Brown, unemployed, who admitted arson and burglary, was jailed for 4½ years.

Search begins for rat army

Council officials are to begin searching today for a pack of 300 rats seen on the move by a nightwatchman before dawn on Saturday in Trowbridge, Wiltshire.

"It was like Hamelin come to life", the watchman said. "These rats were led by a pack of about 20 old stagers, some as big as a decent-sized kitten". They came from the general direction of the town's sewage works or a meat factory, and were last seen heading towards a new superstore.

Vicar fined £20 for poaching a pheasant

Tree man accused

Jonathan Brown, unemployed, who lived in a tree house, was refused bail by magistrates at Evesham, Hereford and Worcester, yesterday when he was accused of stealing a wallet containing £61.

Help for rare birds ends in fire disaster

Mio, Michigan, May 7.—One person died, a dozen houses were burnt down, a thousand people evacuated and 18 square miles of forest destroyed near here yesterday—all to give a bird a nest.

The rare Kirtland Warbler builds its home in pine cones which have been opened by the heat of forest fires.

The state forestry service starts fires every year to ensure it a nesting place. However, this year's blaze went out of control and continued for two days before being extinguished last night.

Hangman halted at last moment

Tehran – A murderer was reprieved at the last moment in a Tehran jail when the mother of his victim decided to forgive him.

Relatives of a murdered person can decide the killer's fate under Islamic law. A prison spokesman was quoted as saying the mother told the hangman to stop as the rope was being placed around the murderer's neck.

Life begins . . .

Reggio Calabria – A 100-year-old woman has been elected to the public health board of the southern Italian town of Taurianova. "I mean to carry out my duties as actively as possible", said Signora Maria Rosa Toscano, a Socialist, accepting the job with enthusiasm.

'Drunk in bus' charge

A bus conductress, of Ladbroke Grove, North Kensington, London, was remanded on bail at Marlborough Street Magistrates' Court yesterday charged with being drunk in a public place, her bus, on New Year's Day.

Prison conception

Berlin, March 13.—A man and a woman, both serving life terms for child murder, have conceived a child inspite of the presence of guards during social periods. The two were married in a West Berlin prison two years ago.

Boy in freezer

The police were investigating alegations yesterday that a boy aged six, needed hospital treatment after his mother locked him in a freezer as punishment. The boy, from the Derby area, is now in the care of the social services department.

Arm sewn back

Mr Gary Bridgstock, a quarry worker, was recovering in Stoke Mandeville Hospital last night after his left arm, which he lost in an accident on Tuesday at a quarry in Corby, had been sewn back in an operation involving microsurgery techniques.

Within the cartoon:

Knife and fork bank threat

Wollongong, Australia, Sept 30.—Harry Fitchett, aged 59, was accused in court here yesterday of trying to rob a bank with a knife and fork.

Two bank cashiers said Mr Fitchett walked into the bank brandishing the cutlery and demanded money. He was found not guilty of demanding money with menaces.

'Dark aliens in UFO' flee from Krugersdorp welcome

THE WAVE of "sightings" of unidentified flying objects sweeping the world since the Christmas photographs of "flying saucers" from New Zealand reached a fresh peak yesterday—an actual "landing."

A former nurse in South Africa claimed to have encountered a pink unidentified object. She said it landed near her home and a squad of strange dark-skinned little men got out.

Mrs Meagan Quezet, of Krugersdorp, west of Johannesburg, said the incident happened just after midnight, when she took her 12-year-old son, Andre, for a walk, because he could not sleep.

"As we walked down the road we could see a bright pink light over a rise and suddenly we came across this thing standing in the road about 20 yards away. In front of it were these five or six beings.

"These people were darkish skinned as far as I could tell. One of the men had a beard and seemed to be the leader.

"I said hello to one of them, but I couldn't understand what he was saying. I told Andre to run off and bring his father and as he did so the creatures jumped about five feet into the air and vanished through a door into their craft.

"The door slid closed and the long steel-type legs began to stretch out. Then with a humming noise, it disappeared into the sky."

Mrs Quezet and her son gave identical descriptions of the craft. They said it had two bright pink lights on either side of the doorway, and its crew appeared to be wearing white or pink suits. One wore a white helmet.

ISRAELI SIGHTINGS
Police alerted

A spate of UFO sightings were also reported from Israel. They ranged from a red ball over Haifa, to sparkling red, blue and purple lights over Jerusalem. The air force said nothing showed up on radar screens.

'Tricks of light'

More reports of UFO poured into Wellington from all over New Zealand yesterday, as two more scientists discounted any sinister aspects of filmed sightings last week.

Pandamonium

UNUSUALLY loud roars from pandas during their mating season are raising hopes that this year will bring a boom in panda births in north-west China, experts say.

Jail for selling baby

Hongkong, March 18.—A man was jailed here for six months for selling his daughter of 20 months for the equivalent of just over £300 to pay gambling debts.

Moving spectacle

PASSENGERS at Heathrow dropped luggage in amazement yesterday at the sight of a couple making love on a moving walkway connecting two of the airport terminals. Some abandoned their suitcases to keep up with events, which began at Terminal Three when a blonde met her boyfriend who had flown in from New York. After seven-and-a-half torrid minutes on the walkway (not counting one gap between two sections) they joined a flight to Paris. An airport official said: "They obviously got carried away."

MARRIAGE No 26 FOR MR WOLFE

Los Angeles

EVERY year Glynn "Scotty" Wolfe renders the GUINNESS BOOK OF RECORDS out of date. He did it again yesterday by announcing that he had married for the 26th time.

And at 75, he set a record of his own. His new bride, Christine Camacho, is 38. None of the others was over 22.

"I feel wonderful," said Mr Wolfe, who this time chose a Las Vegas wedding chapel for the ceremony.

On his way out, someone handed him the GUINNESS BOOK, which lists him as the man with the most marriages in the monogamous world.

"Marriage is the greatest adventure next to death," he said. "It's always fun."

But it is never constant: He was divorced from all previous 23 wives. He married two of them twice.

He was first wed in 1927. His longest marriage lasted nearly five years, while the shortest was 19 days. He has 40 children. The cost has been more than $1m (£714,000) in alimony.

'Loved them all'

"I loved all my wives but we just couldn't get along," he shrugged.

As for his winning, wooing ways, he said: "I'm a gentleman in the parlour; a cook in the kitchen, and a Romeo in the bedroom."

A former miner, pilot, bootlegger and Evangelist, Mr Wolfe now runs a small hotel on the California-Mexico border. For a while he kept a couple of wedding gowns handy in a wardrobe. He has a suitcase crammed with wedding pictures under his bed.

A chapel clerk described his latest bride as "a very nice lady, except she had a lot of tattoos."

Mr Wolfe said he met her 10 years ago. She knows all about him, having met some of his former wives. His only reservation about her, he said, was her habit of eating sunflower seeds in bed.

The seeds of doubt? Last year Mr Wolfe divorced bride number 25 within four months, because she used his toothbrush.

Traffic offence: A runaway hippopotamus from a West German circus attacks a police car before being hustled into a horse van at Kassel.

Eggs and jam

Tokyo, Oct 5.—A lorry carrying eggs collided with another lorry in the Tokyo suburb of Suginami today, and spilt about 66,300 eggs on to the road, suspending traffic for three hours in the morning rush hour. Two fire engines poured sand on the huge pool of egg yolks.

Strawberry war

Mexico City - A quarrel between strawberry growers resulted in 21 deaths and 25 people being wounded by gunfire in the town of Pandicuaro, Michoacan state, police said.

Mayer marriage

Sir Robert Mayer, founder of the Robert Mayer concerts for children, who is 101, married Mrs Jacqueline Noble, his companion, in London yesterday.

WHALE SINKS YACHT

The 41-ft. New Zealand yacht Snow White collided with a whale in the South Pacific yesterday and sank. A Hercules search plane spotted the seven-man crew in two life rafts about 570 miles north of North Cape, and dropped a dinghy, stores and a radio.

HOME FIRE BURNING

Fireman Steve Williams, 29, dashed out on a 999 call yesterday to find his own home in Tudor Road, Weston-super-Mare, Avon, on fire. His wife, Michelle, had escaped from the smoke damaged house, but he had to rescue his sheepdog.

Woman trapped in pit

Mrs Ethel Jones, aged 76, was trapped for an hour yesterday with a broken leg when she fell into a 15 feet pit that opened in the garden of her home in St Paul's Cray, Kent.

Melbourne man accused of jailing children

Melbourne, Nov 7.—Eight children, the eldest of whom is 21, were kept imprisoned in their home from birth because their father believed that the outside world was evil, a police prosecutor told a court yesterday.

When police raided the Melbourne house of Mr Miroslav Kolak, a Yugoslav immigrant, they were forced to scale a 13ft-high fence and penetrate an elaborate security system including searchlights, sirens and electronic eyes.

The prosecutor said the security system was better than that employed in the local prison. Neighbours said they were unaware of the existence of the children until a few weeks before the police raid.

Mr Alexander Kolak, the eldest child, told the court that until July this year he had never been to a doctor or dentist. He escaped from the house with two of his brothers and his 18-year-old sister and reported the situation

Mr Miroslav Kolak, a minister of a local religious sect, was sent for trial on charges of unlawfully imprisoning the four children who escaped.

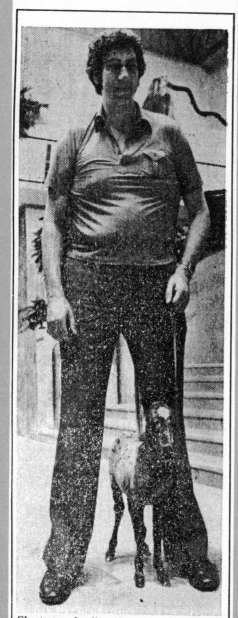

Shortest and tallest: Pegasus, a Falabella horse – the world's smallest breed – stands 17in high at the feet of Britain's tallest man, Mr Chris Greener, whose height is 7ft 6¼in. Both were appearing at the opening of the Guinness World of Records exhibition yesterday at the new three-level Trocadero complex of shops, restaurants and entertainments in Piccadilly Circus, London.

In the wake, or should I say trail, of our recent tale about "super-snail", the mollusc that suddenly came to life after more than three years hibernating as a seaside ornament on the bedroom dressing table of a retired Nottinghamshire miner, I have some new even more startling revelations.

Dr Peter Mordan, senior scientific officer in the zoological department of the British Museum and an expert on non-marine molluscs (land and fresh water snails), tells me of the even more extraordinary achievement of a formidable Egyptian snail, Eremina desertorum.

Apparently in the Annals and Magazine of Natural History of 1850, sandwiched between worthy letters on the breathing habits of spiders and skin shedding in toads, is a short note entitled "Long-suspended vitality of a snail".

This is an account of how in 1846 the British Museum received two specimens of this desert snail which according to the then standard curatorial practice were glued to a small tablet and placed in a collections drawer.

Four years later in March 1850 one of the museum staff suspecting that one of the shells might still be occupied removed it from the tablet and placed it in some tepid water. Much to his surprise and delight it moved.

This hardy little creature apparently lived happily for a further two years after its resurrection.

A JOINT VENTURE

Like any two people who've been going around together for ages, Siamese twins suffer certain schisms. But they stand united on important issues. An affair with a local carpenter when the girls were on show in Vienna in 1910 left Josepha Blazek holding the baby. But her sister was totally supportive – one of those ideal aunties who are always happy to babysit.

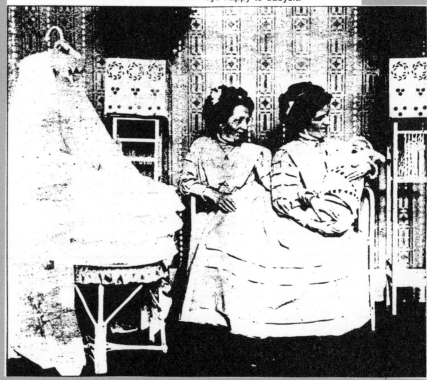

Bird memorized phone number

A lost budgerigar puzzled a family who found it by persistently repeating "223723". Then Mrs Gloria Froggatt, of Minver Crescent, Aspley, Nottingham dialled the figures on her telephone, and the bird's owner answered.

Mrs Muriel Hydes, a widow, of Blandford Road, Chilwell, Nottingham, had taught her pet to repeat the number.

Suicide barrier

A wire barrier has been erected along the 280ft high Clifton suspension bridge in Bristol, from where more than a dozen people have committed suicide in the past year.

End of an affair

Oakland, California – A 70-year-old wife, shot and killed her 72-year-old husband on Christmas Day because he was having an affair with another woman, police said.

Skeletons found

The skeletons of a man and a woman with a child cradled in her arms have been found by workmen renovating a house in Shelley Row, Cambridge. They are thought to be those of a medieval family killed by plague.

He lost his leg, part of his pelvis, his genitals and his rectum. The judge said only 11 people in the world were known to have survived such injuries.

Long way round

Brisbane — The 40-year-old Australian long-distance runner, Ron Grant, a bread saleman, arrived exhausted to a hero's welcome after running 10,364 miles around Australia in 217 days. He wore out 14 pairs of shoes.

Sextuplets stop bus

Guatemala City, Sept 22.— Señora Maria Ixcoy, aged 22, gave birth to sextuplets underneath a bus which made an emergency stop on a rural highway in western Guatemala, hospital officials reported. They said the five boys and a girl were in good condition in hospital here.

On the grass

Peking — A Chinese farm worker who began eating grass six years ago now depends on it for two thirds of his daily food, a Peking newspaper reports. If he omits it from his diet, he gets a splitting headache and in the winter he eats straw.

Hunt deaths

Rome — A huntsman shot his brother dead by mistake near Pesaro, another man was fatally wounded near Pisa and five people are in hospital with gunshot wounds on the first day of the Italian hunting season.

Crash landing

Rome —A Hungarian tourist walking in the Piazza Venezia was badly injured when a suspected thief threw himself from a third-floor window and landed on top of her. The suspect suffered multiple injuries.

The case of the drinking nun

Lorient — A 46-year-old French nun who drove off the road into a ditch after drinking a bottle of port to celebrate the end of an All Saints' Day pilgrimage has been given an eight-day suspended prison sentence for drunken driving.

A court in this western Brittany town also withdrew Sister Anne-Marie Bellesoeur's driving licence for a year. The judge warned her that she would go to jail if she "played the fool again in the next five years".

A fortune gone with the wind

Plattsburgh, New York — A man who threw ripped $100, $50 and $20 notes out his car window, claiming he did not need money, has been arrested.

He was taken to a mental hospital after telling police he had literally thrown away a $20,000 (£13,000) fortune.

80 years late

San Francisco — Lynn Barthel has returned three books, borrowed by her grandmother almost 80 years ago.

Strange case of vanishing house

Phillipsburg, New Jersey — Mr Charles Vosseler and his wife, thinking burglars were breaking into their house when they heard noises in the basement, called the police. But when police arrived they saw the couple run out in their nightclothes as the house began sinking into the ground.

Lieutenant James Macauley said: "We think it was a water main break that caused the earth to swallow the house up. The windows of the top floor were at ground level in a matter of minutes."

PRICKLY CUSTOMER

Mr Ping Law called the police when he discovered a "dangerous animal" in the kitchen of his Chinese restaurant in Sunderland. Police discovered a hedgehog — the first Mr Ping had ever seen.

Dead loss

San Salvador — Police believe relatives exhumed the body of a man illegally to search for a winning $40,000 (£23,000) lottery ticket after a ticket seller arrived at the dead man's home to ask why he had not claimed his prize. The ticket was not found.

Student does 8-hr operation on himself

A STUDENT operated on his own abdomen for eight hours in his college room with an expertise that astonished skilled surgeons, according to the latest *Journal* of the American Medical Association.

The 22-year-old spent months preparing for an operation on his adrenal glands by studying surgical books and acquiring the necessary instruments and medications, writes Dr Ned H. Kalin of the University of Wisconsin Clinical Services Centre in Madison.

He disinfected his room, draped sterilised sheets over his body, swallowed barbiturates for anaesthesia and performed the operation, wearing sterile gloves and a surgical mask.

He kept a canister of vaporised adrenalin at his side in case of shock.

Scalpel and mirrors

"Lying supine and looking into strategically placed mirrors, he began by cleansing his abdomen with alcohol," the article said.

"The incision was made with a scalpel, exposure obtained by retractors, and the dissection carried out with surgical instruments."

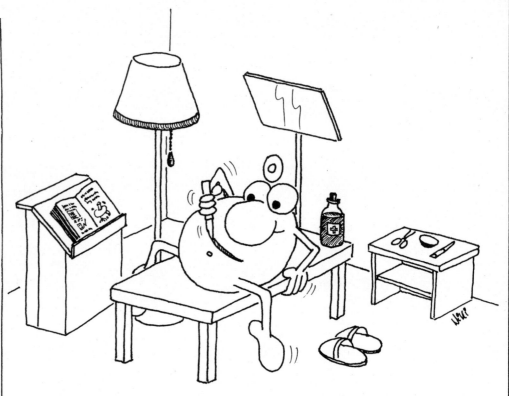

After eight hours, he had to give up because of unexpected pain in retracting his liver. Exhausted, he bandaged his wound, cleaned his room, and called the police.

On arrival at hospital, astonished surgeons examined the man, found his wounds to be remarkably clean and free of infection, discovered gauze bandages packed in his abdomen and noted ligatures tied around major blood vessels. The surgeons closed the wounds and the patient recovered.

Need for psychiatry

Dr Kalin wrote: "He has mastered the concepts and techniques of medicines in an attempt to cure himself, when, in reality, we have little to offer him that would result in effective treatment."

Dr Kalin recommended the patient undergo extensive psychiatric counselling.

School 'kidnap' ends in police swoop

A sixth-form mock kidnap went badly wrong for five boys dressed in military clothes and brandishing toy guns yesterday.

The police were called and within minutes three squad cars, a van and Scotland Yard's new helicopter went to the rescue of Mr James Parson, deputy headmaster of Kelsey School for Boys, Beckenham, London.

Instead of holding him to "ransom" to raise funds for the Spastics Society, the boys were surrounded, forced to lie down and bundled into the police van.

Deep thinker

New Plymouth

Explaining why he would not be seeking reelection to Stratford council in New Zealand's North Island, after 12 years service, Mr Gerald Gower stated: "I can only say that when I works I works hard, when I sits I sits loose, when I thinks I falls asleep. As a councillor one must both sit and think".

Readers' errors

Palermo, Feb 3.—Two men looking at newspapers in a bank queue in Palermo were arrested because they were known to be illiterate, police said. They had guns and were about to rob the bank.

Motoring record

Mr Robert Burnett, of Wallasey, Merseyside, has passed a driving test at the age of 85 years and nine months, which is two months older than the previous record in the *Guinness Book of Records*.

Tongue saved

Police constable Paul Allen yesterday saved the life of Paul Jerome, 18, after he had swallowed his tongue during a fight outside the football club at Reading, Berkshire. The policeman had his fingers bitten, but managed to pull the youth's tongue from his throat and called an ambulance.

Dolphins 'save ferry boys'

Jakarta, Feb 2.—Three children on the Indonesian passenger liner Tampomas II that sank last Tuesday in the Java Sea, killing 140 people, were rescued by dolphins, the Jakarta newspaper *Berita Buana* reported.

When their father threw the three boys from the burning ferry into the sea, a group of dolphins immediately came and pushed them towards a lifeboat, the newspaper added. Their parents are still missing.

The Indonesian Government decided today to resume its abandoned search and rescue operations after the discovery this weekend of 109 survivors on Doang-Doangan island.—

£2m error

New York - Two doctors who told a patient he had three months to live must pay $3.1m (about £2m) for wrongly diagnosing his illness as cancer, then treating him with powerful drugs that may put him at risk of leukaemia. He turned out to have inflammation of the colon.

TV in a tent

Peking Nomadic herdsmen in China's remote Qinghai Province can now buy waterproof, antiseptic tents instead of the fetid yak-hide yurts they have lived in for centuries, the New China news agency said. One herdsman hopes to watch television on a set run off a wind-driven generator.

Shark used as rates cheque

Mr James Sullivan, a Cornish fishmonger, yesterday paid his rates with a cheque written on the belly of an 8ft, 350 lb shark, because his local council had refused permission for a fish and chip counter at his shop.

After close examination by staff at Caradon District Council's office in Liskeard, the shark was taken by council van to the Midland Bank, where the £222.71 amount due was credited to the council's account.

Elephant has tooth filled

Bloemfontein — It took 17 dentists, doctors, veterinarians and technicans and enough anesthetic to kill 70 men to cure Homly, a 60-year-old Asian elephant cow of her toothache. A large cavity in a molar, about the size of a man's fist, was successfully filled with amalgam and the patient eventually woke up and walked about.

The operation involved continuous heart monitoring and blood tests as the 3.5 milligrams of an anesthetic similar to morphine — about 0.05 is normally enough to kill a man — was administered.

'I killed 156'

Austin, Texas - A wandering handyman, Henry Lee Lucas, already indicted on six murder counts, now says he killed 156 people. The *American-Statesman* reported. His details of the killings are so vivid that police are not doubting him.

Puppy calls 999

Bruno, a mongrel puppy, caused a police alert yesterday when it knocked over a push-button telephone at its home in Fareham, Hampshire, and punched the 9 button three times with its paw.

Chain collision

Manila, March 11.—A speeding lorry hit a delivery van, triggering a chain collision of 24 other vehicles that injured 17 people, two seriously, on an expressway south of Manila.

Sharp practice

Honolulu - Carpet tacks strewn along the cycling route may have wrecked the chances of more than 100 competitors in last weekends Iron Man triathlon world championships in Hawaii the 1981 champion, John Howard (US), was among those knocked out by a puncture. Police are investigating.

SCHOOLBOY HOAX WINS DAY OFF

A boy fed up with trudging to school in cold weather telephoned to the BBC, impersonated his headmaster, and convinced Radio Norfolk to broadcast that Northgate High in East Dereham, had been closed because of weather conditions.

Mr John Gibbs, the headmaster, heard the broadcast and managed to get a correction, but it was too late and more than 500 of the 700 children stayed away. The BBC apologised yesterday and promised that it would never happen again.

GIRLFRIEND KILLED AND EATEN

Paris, June 16

A Japanese student has told Paris police that he shot his Dutch girlfriend and ate part of her because she refused to make love to him.

Issei Sagawa, aged 32, was arrested early today after the girl's body was found cut up and stuffed into two suitcases in the Bois de Boulogne. He told police that after his girl had turned him down, he shot her and put bits from her body in a refrigerator. He said he had always wanted to eat a young woman.

The final shift

Stulln.—A Bavarian chemical works plunged 70ft into a mine below its foundations. Ten workers got out in time to see the plant swallowed in a crater 50 yards wide.

Jailer critical after fall into hot porridge

Durban — A South African prison warder was in critical condition in hospital yesterday after falling into a cauldron of boiling corn porridge, the Prisons Service said.

The warder, Sibusiso Mkhize, aged 30, inadvertently fell into the cauldron while working in a prison kitchen. "The top half of his body was submerged," a prisons spokesman said.

Foul play was not suspected by the prison authorities.

SHERRY IS MY MEDICINE, SAYS MAN OF 107

Mr Alfie Grant, who will be 108 in April, revealed the secret of his long life yesterday: 6 double sherries and 10 cigarettes a day. Every day he walks the 400 yards from an old people's home at Dovercourt, near Harwich, to the Royal public house.

Mr Grant, a bachelor, said "Shery is my medicine. I like a smoke, too, but I stick to 10 a day because people say it is bad for you."

Mr Jim Hughes, landlord of the Royal, said "Alfie costs me a bomb because I still serve him double sherries at 30p a glass, and the real price is £1·20."

Wing and a . . .

Phoenix — Mrs Editha Merrill, aged 78, with no flight training, landed a single-engine aircraft safely here after the pilot died. Sitting in the co-pilot's seat, she took over the controls and followed instructions from the pilot's wife in the back seat. "I did an awful lot of praying", she said.

Death defied

Innsbruck —An Austrian skydiver survived a 3,300ft plunge after his parachutes malfunctioned. Gerhard Marinell, aged 42, crashed on to a roof in Soelden, near Innsbruck, before falling into a garden about 8ft below. He broke his ribs in the fall.

About-face

New York — The author of the best-selling book *How to Make Love to a Woman* Michael Morgenstern, has been ordered to stand trial next week for allegedly punching his girlfriend in the face after finding her in their flat with another man.

Last word

Peking — Wang Lian, who cut out his wife's tongue and then pleaded guilty to charges of "cruelly mistreating" her, was executed on Sunday in Liaoning province. His attitude to women was widespread, even among Communist Party cadres, the local paper commented.

Man bites dog

Jakarta — An enraged villager killed a dog by sinking his teeth into its throat after it bit a six-year-old boy.

Rat race

Jakarta — A village chief in West Java is charging couples 10 dead rats to get married — and 25 for a divorce.

Killer piano

San Francisco —A man reclining with a woman on top of a piano at a topless nightclub was crushed to death when the piano was raised to the ceiling as part of the show. The woman escaped through a ceiling hatch.

Crowded sky

Sioux Falls, South Dakota — A Republic Airlines plane, its tail emblazoned with the stylized goose that is its symbol, met the real thing head on as it approached Sioux Falls. A goose crashed through the cockpit windscreen, injuring the pilot but the co-pilot landed the airliner safely.

Dead drunk by the swag

Police tipped off about a housebreaking found a man passed out in an easy chair with an empty bottle of whisky by his side in Johannesburg yesterday. The owners of the house are on holiday.

The man's pockets were stuffed with jewelry and there was a bag of swag ready to be taken away. When he came to in the police station he was arrested.

Baby survives

Las Vegas — A baby delivered six weeks prematurely after her mother committed suicide was reported to be in a critical but stable condition in hospital here. Doctors worked frantically for two hours to save the life of 5lb 8oz Emily Tippetts, who was delivered by Caesarean section.

Gold diggers

Manila — Prostitutes working among itinerant gold prospectors in the southern Philippines are insisting on payment in gold dust or nuggets and refusing paper money because the peso is threatened with further devaluation.

IT'S BUGGY LONGLEGS

What has six legs, stands 19ft. tall, and scares the daylights out of you alongside Highway 395 in Reno, Nevada? It's called The Beetle, and took sculptor David Anthony Fambrough five months to create. It is pictured here in its natural habitat – behind Mr Fambrough's Reno antique shop.

The Volkswagen body elevated in this extraordinary fashion is one manifestation of Mr Fambrough's curious weekend hobby. A remodelled 1929 Dodge, now transformed into a tarantula, is another. A 25ft. steel flower with 8ft. butterflies made from horseshoes is also on view.

A VW dealer is reported to be interested in The Beetle, for sale for much more than the price of a new car. The tarantula has no takers as yet, but this does not deter the ambitious Mr F, who is even now planning his next *oeuvre:* turning a train into a centipede.

HEDGEHOGS GET GREEN LIGHT

Families were mystified by tiny flashing lights in the darkness. They were even more puzzled when they investigated and saw hedgehogs with green, red and silver lights in their spines.

Carole Hughes, a schoolgirl, of Meadow End, Radcliffe on Trent, Nottinghamshire, said yesterday : " I saw one with a silver light fitted to its back and another with a red flashing light ".

Later the mystery was solved. Dr Christopher Barnard, zoology lecturer at Nottingham University, said his staff had fitted the lights to 30 hedgehogs to monitor their mating habits.

Grave error

Hongkong — The Government said it made a mistake when the official gazette announced a contract to build an indoor recreation centre in Happy Valley Cemetery. The centre would actually be built under an elevated highway opposite the Happy Valley race course.

Healer arrested

Bogota, April 27.—Police have arrested a faith healer after the death of a girl, aged 12, who was sealed in the belly of a slaughtered steer for six hours in order to exorcise demons, a press report said.

Jailhouse stew

Cadiz (AFP). — Warders at Cadiz Prison had to lock prisoners in their cells to fend off protests after the cook was accused of urinating in a stew pot.

Passengers flee as orang-utan catches the bus

Bangkok, Nov 22.—When an orang-utan, lamenting the loss of his mate, boarded a crowded Bangkok bus, all the passengers decided it was time to get off.

The shrieking exodus from the bus must have left the 20-year-old orang-utan even lonelier because he immediately clambered off the bus to assuage his hurt feelings with a bunch of bananas stolen from a roadside vendor.

But as he looked for a friend to share his bananas, his search for companionship was coming quickly to an end, for hot on his trail were keepers from Dusit zoo where his morning stroll had begun some hours before.

Apparently frustrated by limited opportunities to meet young female orang-utans at the zoo, he used stones thrown into his cage to smash his way through a wall.

Girl aged 10 makes her debut as playwright

A north London schoolgirl aged 10 is to have *Perfect Pigs,* her first play, given a professional production at the Royal Court's Theatre Upstairs next month, as part of the 1981 Young Writers' Festival.

Swans interrupt road work

Swans nesting in the middle of the route of the new Beccles by-pass in Norfolk are to be protected.

Mr Ian Sutherland, the resident engineer, said yesterday : " We will stop work and start again the other side of the nest. When all seven eggs have hatched and the cygnets have gone we will build the rest of the road and embankment."

Pigs ahoy

Apia, Western Samoa – About 300 pigs living on Fakaofo atoll in the Tokelau Islands of the South Pacific have learnt to swim and fish, living on a diet of seaslugs, small molluscs and fish.

Slow getaway

Police in Ferndown, Dorset, followed a trail of broken milk bottles left by thieves who stole a safe containing £300 from a dairy, then used a milk float to get away. It was found abandoned later.

Nightcap

Paris – Regine Le Guilloux, mother of seven grown-up sons, was detained awaiting trial on a charge of putting sleeping pills in her husband's soup every night so that he would not want sexual relations with her.

High-level diplomacy

President Abdou Diouf of Senegal, who is 6ft 8in tall, towering over Mr Pierre Trudeau, the Canadian Prime Minister, who is 11 inches shorter, before the two sat down to a working lunch in Ottawa.

Fatal error

Porto Ferrario, Italy — Herr Manfred Koberle, aged 22, a German tourist lying in a fur sleeping bag was shot dead on the island of Elba by a man who mistook him for a wild boar, police reported yesterday.

The exploding Easter eggs

Lerouville, France – A woman trying to prepare Easter eggs upset her neighbours by putting a pot on the stove to boil, forgetting about it and going to bed.

When the boiling water evaporated, the eggs shattered, causing a series of small detonations. Thinking their village was being attacked, her neighbours armed themselves with guns and sticks until police arrived.

Mouseburger

Riverside, California – A man who was ill after ordering a hamburger at a fast-food restaurant here, sent an uneaten portion to the county health department for analsis. It was found to contain mouse brain, mouse liver and mouse fur and his legal action was settled out of court.

Finger tip-off traps muggers

Hong Kong – A man walked into a police station here, reported an attempted mugging and handed over his evidence, a finger tip, which he said he had bitten off one of his attackers.

After seeking hospital treatment for a shortened index finger, a man was detained and another later arrested.

The biter bit

Richmond, South Africa – A 14-year-old black herdboy bit a 16ft python to death after it attacked him last week, police in this rural eastern town said.

Red faces

Alfred, Ontario

Red-faced firemen had to watch their village fire station burn down here because an electrical failure jammed the door and they could not get their fire engines out.

Are they twins? : Mr Robert Shafran (left) and Mr Eddy Galland, both aged 19, met each other for the first time at Liberty, New York and both gasped with surprise. Mr Shafran had enrolled at a college where Mr Galland had been a student before he withdrew from his course. The greetings from other students for Mr Shafran were warm and enthusiastic but everyone addressed him as "Eddy". Eventually, through a third party, the two were brought together. They believe they are twins, who were separated at birth—both were adopted as infants but know nothing of their natural parents.

Cow razes farm

The Hague, Sept 27.—Gas from a cow's stomach burned down a farm near here today. A veterinary surgeon inserted a tube into the stomach and lit a match to test the gas. The resulting explosion set fire to bales of hay and the flames spread.

KISSERS CALLED TO ACCOUNT

KISSING, hugging and the other unseemly, unmanly acts which take place on the football field when goals are scored should cease forthwith, FIFA, world soccer's governing body, is urging.

Instead, FIFA wants a return to those corinthian days of yore when players with baggy sharts and centre partings shook hands and exchanged a brief "Well played, Fred," and "Nice shot, Cyril," after the ball had burst the back of the net to the acclaim of thousands following a pitch-length, defence splitting move which won the match in the last minute.

"We feel that the scorer should be congratulated by the team captain or the player who made the pass," says an editorial in this month's FIFA NEWS.

"The exultant outbursts of several players at once jumping on top of each other, kissing and embracing is really excessive and inappropriate and should be banned."

TRAGEDY OF ROPE TRICK

An escapologist fell 60ft to his death during his first public performance of a new stunt, an inquest heard yesterday.

The rope burnt through because he did not realize that he had to soak it in water to repel the paraffin, Mr John Glanville, the Portsmouth Coroner, said. He recorded a verdict of misadventure.

Foot in Moscow arms talks

Youth's feet sewn on after accident

Peter Holmes, aged 17, of Hastings Road, Northampton, had both his feet sewn on yesterday after they had been amputated by the blades of a soapmixing machine he was cleaning at Nimbus Laboratories, Northampton.

After an all-night operation a spokesman at Stoke Mandeville hospital said the operation had been successful and his condition was satisfactory. Mr Holmes was working at the factory on a scheme under the youth opportunities programme.

Boy kills sister

Indianapolis.—A three-year-old boy shot dead his baby sister with a Magnum revolver he found in a drawer at his grandfather's home.

Doctor who said 'hit patient with bottle' is cleared

A doctor called out at 3 am to attend a dying man aged 90 told relatives to hit him over the head with a bottle, the General Medical Council was told yesterday.

He told the council's disciplinary committee in London that he was trying to be light-hearted and strike up a rapport with the family.

The committee dismissed the charge.

Spun coin decides jail term

New York, Feb 2

A controversial New York judge has decided a jail sentence for a pickpocket on the toss of a coin. At Manhattan Criminal Court Judge Alan Friess proposed 30 days for the youth, who had pleaded guilty. The defendant Jeffery Jones, aged 18, said he thought 20 days would be a fairer sentence.

"Is your client a gambling man?" the judge asked Mr Jones's lawyer, Mr Michael Muscato. The judge then asked Mr John Jordan, Assistant District Attorney, for a 25 cent coin and ordered the defendant to make the toss, and call. The pickpocket called tails, and won.

Judge Friess, who caused a furore last year by releasing a woman murder suspect without bail and taking her home, imposed a 20-day sentence.

He had originally offered three years' probation to Mr Jones, who told the judge he was already on a year's probation for a similar offence and wanted to do the time in jail.

Japan using robots to produce robots

Boy shot dead

Stanton, California (AP) – A police officer killed a five-year-old boy who had a toy pistol on Thursday. He opened fire after seeing a figure in the dark holding a gun.

A dog's revenge

When a dog was knocked down at a road junction in Sheffield the car stopped and the dog ran back, jumped and bit the passenger. The dog was unhurt.

Fizz feud

Bangkok.—A Pepsi-Cola employee in northern Thailand was shot dead by a Coca-Cola employee after an argument over who would get the space in front of a restaurant for advertisement posters.

Whaler captain goes down with his ship

Funchal, Madeira, July 25.— The Norwegian captain of a Dutch whaler that capsized as it was pulling a giant whale on board went down with his ship with a beer in his hand, survivors said today.

The 42 crew of the 543-ton factory ship Tonna, registered in the Dutch Antilles, were landed here early this morning after being picked up by the 4,712-ton Greek cargo ship Gomasa when the whaler foundered last Saturday some 220 miles off the Portuguese coast.

They said the last thing they saw before the ship went down was Captain K. Vesprhein, aged 52, clinging to the bridge with a beer to his lips. They implored him to abandon ship but he refused to leave his post.

A Highgate colleague, who walks his mongrel in Parkland Walk, a former railway line become a meeting place for dog-owners and their mutts, encountered a couple who proudly told him about their doberman pincher.

Returning home one night they found a round hole in the kitchen window and the young dog writhing and choking on the floor. They rushed to the vet who, to their surprise, extricated three human fingers from the doberman's throat.

They telephoned all the hospitals to say that if anyone was missing three fingers they could be reclaimed from the vet, but no one reported his loss to the casualty departments.

Arm stitched back

Ryan Millard, aged 22 months, was last night chattering to his parents in Withington Hospital, Manchester, only hours after surgeons, using the latest techniques, stitched his arm back on. The baby's pram was crushed by a tractor near his home in Dalton, Cumbria.

War on gobbledegook

The National Consumer Council has declared war on Civil Service jargon and is issuing stickers for people to fix to difficult forms saying: "This is gobbledegook. Please use plain English" A council report says Britain's 100,000 official forms are mostly awful. It is to hold training courses to help bureaucrats.

Sextuplets mystery

Mystery surrounds the reported birth in Cape Town last October of sextuplets to a white girl aged 17. One baby was said to have arrived 23 days after the other five, but so far none has appeared in public.

Invisible art

Dublin Corporation is to pay £20,000 for a new work of art, an apparently blank canvas by Agnes Martin, an American, that was exhibited in the Irish capital recently.

Eric Kenneth Williams, aged 36, a street trader, who was said to have bitten off a taxi driver's ear and part of his thumb, was jailed at the Central Criminal Court yesterday for 18 months.

Mr Williams, of Kennedy Road, Hanwell, was found guilty of maliciously wounding Mr David Bumpstead, aged 45, of Severn Drive, Enfield.

Amusement park 'dummy' was a corpse

Long Beach, California, Dec 9.—A dummy hanging by a noose at the Long Beach Pike Amusement Park has turned out to be a corpse.

The figure had been part of a "fun house" exhibit for five years. Officials at the park discovered that it was a corpse during the filming of an episode of the *Six Million Dollar Man* television show.

A film crewman was adjusting the arm of the dummy when it fell off. On examination a protruding bone was noted and he identified the dummy as a human body.

Authorities described the corpse as an elderly man, 5ft 3in tall and weighing 150lb, but could not say when he died.

The figure, wrapped in gauze and sprayed with fluorescent paint, had been bought by the amusement park from a local wax museum, according to the *Los Angeles Times*.

Officials from the coroner's office said the body was well-preserved "like a mummy and quite leathery".

One of the photographs of the monster taken on board the trawler.

A monster from depths of Pacific

Tokyo, July 20.—Japanese fishermen caught a dead monster, weighing two tons and 30ft in length, off the coast of New Zealand in April, it was reported today.

Believed to be a survivor of a prehistoric species, the monster was caught at a depth of 1,000ft off the South Island coast, near Christchurch.

Palaeontologists from the National Science Museum in Tokyo have concluded that the beast belonged to the plesiosaurus family—huge, small-headed reptiles with a long neck and four fins. Other scientists said the creature might be "some sort of dinosaur or Loch Ness-type monster."

After a member of the crew had photographed and measured it, the trawler's captain ordered the corpse to be thrown back into the sea because of the fear of contamination to his fish

The company which chartered the trawlers has ordered other vessels in the area to try to find the carcass or, if possible, capture a live specimen.

Michihiko Yano, the crew member who took the photographs, said at a press conference in Tokyo that it would be difficult to recover the carcass because the creature would be almost totally decomposed by now.

He recalled that when it was hoisted on board the trawler, a cable round its abdomen had cut through the body which oozed a white slimy fluid.

The photographs show an animal with white and red skin hanging from its bones.

Mr Yano said : "Some of the crew thought it was a whale, others a turtle without a shell. Some joked that it was a monster. I'm not sure what it was, but it does look like drawings I saw of Nessie after my return home last month."

Marine biologists such as Professor Fujio Yasuda of Tokyo Fisheries University are also undecided. But they are fairly certain that it was not a whale, turtle, seal, dolphin or shark.

Severed foot is sewn on again

La Spezia, Italy, Nov 6.—A British sailor whose foot was cut off here has had it sewn on again, hospital officials said.

Mr Richard Pickett, aged 23, from London, had his left foot severed by steel cable being winched across the deck of a yacht.

Happy choice of words by Victor Bradley, secretary of the Reigate Cesspit Users' Association, reported in the Surrey Mirror. Announcing a public meeting to complain about the council's charges to cesspit users, he said : "We want to give the problem an airing without raising a stink."

Hairy tale

THE infant son of a peasant couple in Liaoning Province has hair everywhere on his body except his palms, his soles, and the tip of his nose, reports the New China News Agency. Scientists and doctors have made a film about Yu Chen-huan called "hair-covered baby boy" the agency said.

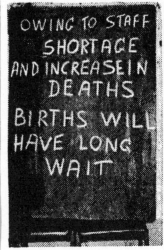

Today's macabre sign was photographed at Paddington Register Office.

Doctor eats deadly mushrooms

Geneva, Sept 15.—A French family doctor who today ate a lunch of deadly poisonous mushrooms to prove he had discovered the antidote, was sleeping peacefully tonight.

Dr Pierre Bastien, aged 57, from Remieremont in eastern France ate in the restaurant of Swiss Television after Geneva University and the World Health Organization refused permission for the experiment on their premises.

A cook sautéd 70 grams (2.5 oz) of the Death Cap mushroom (Amanita Phalloides) in butter at the doctor's instructions.

He experienced stomach pains during the evening but these went after he took the antidote at 9.15 pm.

MAN BITES WIFE IN DOG DREAM

Jerusalem, Jan 5

The "man bites dog" formula was taken to new limits today by the Hebrew newspaper *Yediot Ahronot* which reported that a man arrested in Tel Aviv for biting his wife told the police that he had dreamt he was a dog.

The man aged 73 hurt his 70-year-old wife so seriously while she was sleeping at 2 am today that she had to be treated in hospital. He said he could remember only that he had dreamt he was a dog.

Python problem

Philadelphia.—A man who carried a python in a bag as protection against robbers was arrested for recklessly endangering another person on Thursday night, after the snake bit a policeman, who beat it to death with his truncheon.

Cyst outweighed the patient

A childless married woman aged 44 from Bristol has had an ovarian cyst removed which weighed more than she did. The cyst, removed at Frenchay Hospital, Bristol, weighed 9 stones 8lb, and the woman weighed 9 stones 7lb after the operation.

She had a swelling of the abdomen for five years but had not sought help because of a fear of doctors. Eventually her doctor visited and persuaded her to go into hospital, where nine gallons of fluid was drained off and the cyst removed.

Finger bitten off

Hongkong, July 3.—A housewife who bit off the finger of a woman neighbour during a quarrel has been sentenced to three months' imprisonment.

Maggot rivals blamed for raid on farm

Raiders who broke into a maggot farm at Darlton, near Newark, Nottinghamshire, yesterday, drugged two guard dogs and used insect spray to kill millions of bluebottles.

Mr Philip Bland, the owner, said: "Every bluebottle was dead.

"It was a professional job. I believe it was rival maggot producers who want to push up the price by putting me out of business."

Another maggot farm near Doncaster has also been raided and both breeders are offering a £5,000 joint reward.

Hotfoot to hospital

George Robert Mills, aged 29, a mechanic from London, was recovering in Athens yesterday from third-degree burns after watching a traditional firewalking ceremony at Langada, northern Greece. He apparently thought the ceremony was a fake, took off his shoes and jumped on to the hot coals.

Forty years on

A former soldier has written to the police admitting that he was the man who climbed the Corn Exchange clock tower at Chard, Somerset, 41 years ago and stopped the clock. The police have cautioned him.

Surprise brew

Toronto, Feb 8.—A court here ordered a brewery to pay $1,500 (£850) damages to a man who said he found a dead mouse in his bottle of beer.

WEDDING SHOCK FOR GUEST

A man who went to a register office on Saturday to witness a wedding ceremony came out a married man. Mr Peter Graddon, aged 25, of Estover, Plymouth, went to the office because his girl friend Miss Julie Brain, had told him a relative of hers was renewing her marriage vows.

But when he got there Miss Brain, aged 26, was wearing bride's attire. She handed in a special marriage licence and wedding ring, and they were married. After the wedding, at Plymouth, Peter said: "I was absolutely shocked. We have wanted to get married for a long time, but we couldn't afford it."

His bride said: "Things changed before Christmas when Peter's father and mother heard of our problems and offered to pay almost the whole cost of the wedding. We then jointly agreed to give Peter a surprise."

A FATEFUL FRIDAY

Mr Robert Renphrey, a bus conductor, who claims to be the most accident-prone man in Britain, spent yesterday, Friday the thirteenth, in bed.

In the past five years Mr Renphrey, aged 53, of Fletton Avenue, Peterborough, has been involved in five car crashes and four bus breakdowns, has fallen into a river, been knocked down by a motorcycle and has walked through a plate glass door.

A SECOND AHEAD

Washington, June 18.—June 30 will be one second longer this year to get in step with the Earth's rotation, the United States Commerce Department said.

It explained that the Earth's rotation, on which solar time is based, is not as regular as the atomic clocks used by scientists. So-called leap seconds were introduced in 1972 to keep atomic clocks from getting ahead or behind solar time.—

The train arriving . . .

Helsinki.—John Massis, a Belgian, has set a new world record here by towing a 136-ton train for 1.26 metres with his teeth.

Mother's revenge

Lübeck, March 6.—A woman entered a West German court today, pulled out a revolver and shot dead a butcher aged 35 on trial for murdering her seven-year-old daughter.

Dog's life of disasters

A third-party insurance policy taken out for £17 by Mr and Mrs John Green, of Torquay, on their accident prone dog, paid off yesterday.

Monty, a 13-month-old boxer, was tied to a grocer's vegetable rack when he chased a cat, dragging the rack with him, denting one car and smashing another's headlight. The bill is £150.

BITE FOILS TIGER

A woman saved her 10-year-old daughter by biting a tiger in Kuwait Zoo, the Kuwaiti newspaper AL-QABAS reported yesterday. When the tiger reached from its cage and got the child's head between its paws, the mother bit it and pulled the girl free.

Transatlantic barrel boat burnt on beach

Mr Edward McNamara, who on Tuesday called off his attempt to cross the Atlantic in a glass-fibre barrel, burnt his "boat" yesterday after being talked out of making another attempt by a vicar and lifeboatmen.

He sipped champagne as he celebrated his sixty-first birthday and watched his vessel being reduced to ashes on the beach at Sennen Cove, Land's End.

On Tuesday he had to abandon his venture after only 50 minutes as he was repeatedly rolled out of the barrel.

He added that he would reconsider the project and might make another attempt.

School horror

Bangkok — Three children were killed and 16 wounded when an automatic rifle being demonstrated by a policeman at a school at Tambon Smakkhi jerked out of control and sprayed bullets into the playground crowd.

The other casualties . . .

PRINCE PHILIP spoke today about another casualty of the Falklands conflict—the whale population of the South Atlantic.

He said he assumed a great many whales had been mistaken for submarines by the British Task Force and had been destroyed.

IN THE now-famous film of the Princes Gate embassy battle, the explosion of the SAS grenades could be seen to startle a bird which streaked across the screen in the direction of Hyde Park. This, I am told, was a Serpentine duck, which had been nesting on a window sill a couple of houses down the row. When the human inhabitants of the house were evacuated, friends of the duck expressed concern that any unseemly commotion might so startle the ducklings that they would tumble off the ledge. So, ever obliging, the police laid foam-rubber matting in the basement area beneath the window. Happily, I hear, the duck has now returned to find its brood intact.

Turtle island turns turtle

Dar es Salaam. — Maziwi Island, off north Tanzania, which was the main nesting place for sea turtles along the East African coast has disappeared beneath the sea, the Tanzanian *Daily News* reports. Two researchers could find no trace of it nor of the turtles.

Carlo forte

Monforte d'Alba Signor Carlo Rappalino, a 90-year-old farmer, beat 40 younger participants in the annual screaming contest in this Piedmont town, his voice booming to 124 decibels. A normal conversation is at 50 decibels.

Woman has baby after womb is removed

A WOMAN in Auckland has made medical history in New Zealand by giving birth to a normal 5lb baby girl nearly nine months after she had had a hysterectomy.

Doctors say Mrs Margaret Martin became pregnant about two days before the operation last September, and a fertilised egg was already on its way from the ovary to the womb.

The egg attached itself to her bowel and other organs inside her abdomen, and the foetus grew and survived.

Mr Greg Martin, 30, said he and his wife, 29, had not known she was pregnant until two months ago. "We didn't know whether to laugh or cry," he said.

Attached to bowel

Dr P. Jackson said at the National Women's Hospital that the egg had fallen out of Mrs Martin's fallopian tube during her hysterectomy. The size of a pinhead, it had attached itself to her bowel where it was nourished by the bowel's blood supply.

Five months later, doctors found a "mass" in Mrs Martin's stomach and were shocked to detect a baby's heartbeat.

The main danger facing the foetus had been starvation, Dr Jackson said, "We were also worried about the possible lack of protection for the baby because it was not surrounded by the womb," he added.

Last month Mrs Alison Trott, 23, of Norton Fitzwarden, Somerset, gave birth to a boy 11 months after she had had a sub total hysterectomy. Doctors did not remove the neck of her womb.

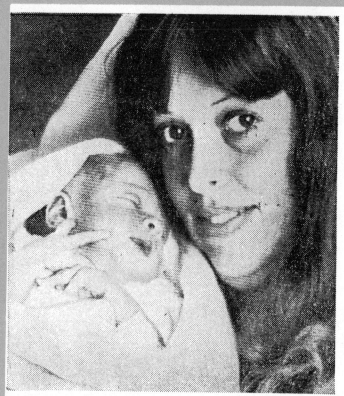

Mrs Margaret Martin with the baby daughter born in Auckland, New Zealand, eight months after a hysterectomy.

Unexpected kittens put doctor in court

A DOCTOR who could not bear to be parted from his pet cat in quarantine substituted a stray he had bought for £5 from the RSPCA when he visited it, a court was told yesterday.

The swap was disovered when the substitute cat gave birth to kittens, for the original had been spayed and all the tomcats in the kennels had been neutered, said Mr JOHN SMYTH, Q.C., at Winchester Crown Court. "You can imagine the consternation," he said.

He was prosecuting Dr PETER HOLDEN, of Barrowfield Drive, Hove, Sussex, who denies removing his cat, Biba, from Kitcombe Kennels, Farringdon, Hants, with intent to avoid anti-rabies regulations.

Mr Smyth said Dr Holden emigrated with his wife to Africa in 1976 taking Biba with them. On their return in April, 1978, they had to put the cat in quarantine for six months.

The substitute cat was sufficiently similar for the Kennels staff to be deceived and Dr Holden would have "got clean away with it" but for the bad luck that it was pregnant.

'Strict precautions'

The birth of kittens caused tremendous excitement in the kennels. "Records showed Biba had been spayed and unless the vet had slipped up clearly something had gone badly wrong," said Mr Symth.

The strictest precautions were taken in the kennels to keep animals apart but cats became pregnant at the drop of a hat.

But the gestation period for cats was 60 to 70 days and it was realised that Biba had been admitted some 90 days before the birth.

The second cat also had a chronic disease and liked chicken mince, which Biba refused.

Dr Holden denies making the swap. He said he bought the second cat as a present for his wife until Biba returned at the end of the quarantine period.

The hearing was adjourned until today.

Lions eat woman alive

Tallassee, Alabama, Oct 24.— Mrs Margaret Hanie, aged 28, was eaten alive by two lions which her husband had bought from a Florida zoo.

Bride shot

Beletweyne, Somalia, Oct 25.—An 18-year-old bride was shot in the head at her wedding by a group of enthusiastic well-wishers who fired into the air.

OH, NO, BROWN COW

A brown cow in the Italian Alpine village of Soldo swallowed a jacket with the equivalent of £4,500 in its pockets. It belonged to a local hotel owner who left his jacket in a cowshed while visiting a farmer.

The fiery cat

Hagi, Japan, Nov 7.—Police investigating a fire which destroyed an historic house here have accused Mr Hiroshi Fujishima, aged 40, a painter, of causing the blaze by setting alight a stray cat which was bothering him in his flat. The animal fled in flames into the house near by.

Lethal umbrella

Pensacola, Florida, Aug 28.— A large beach umbrella blown through the air by a gust of wind impaled a two-year-old Florida boy and killed him.

Can of worms

Cologne — A worm breeder's wife who blames the city of Cologne for the loss of a million worms is seeking more than £100,000 in damages. She says the worms wriggled off when on loan for an experiment because they were not fed properly.

Former slave dies at 121

Chicago — A former slave born two months after the American Civil War began has died here aged 121. Documents produced by the family of Mary Duckworth gave her birth date as June 4, 1861, in Mississippi. She leaves 300 descendants.

T-SHIRT FOR TWO

Two fishermen whose boat was wrecked in a typhoon off the Philippines last week said in Manila yesterday that they survived four days in the sea by eating a T-shirt piece by piece as they trod water. One man died in the shipwreck, seven are missing.

Grim revenge

Namur, Belgium — When neighbours shot a dog owned by Gerard Dauphin, aged 21, because it raided a chicken run, Dauphin took a terrible revenge. He shot dead all four of the family next door, including two children. Yesterday, he was jailed for life.

RAIN OF FROGS

Frogs rained down on the village of Darganata on the Amu Darya river in Soviet Central Asia, Tass news agency reported yesterday. It said the phenomenon was caused by whirlwinds.

Lone attempt to swim Channel ends in rescue

An attempt by Mr Martin Lewis, aged 43, to swim the Channel without a support boat, with just an inner tube to support him and a bicycle torch to warn shipping, ended yesterday three miles out of Dover.

Mr Lewis, a forklift truck driver, of Pulborough Avenue, Eastbourne, who was towing a bag containing his clothes, was lifted into a lifeboat.

He told his rescuers that he had set out from Dover three hours earlier.

Mr Lewis has made other eccentric attempts to cross the Channel. All have failed. In 1971 he and his wife and another couple set off on a 40-foot raft of oil drums powered by an old Ford car. They had to be rescued.

Whisky bequest

Mr Leonard Botham, of Totteridge Village, North London, who died in May, left 100 bottles of Teacher's whisky to Mr Cyril Kostoris, of Cowden, Kent, " in memory of the thousands we have drunk together "

Scalp reform

Peking — Chinese Buddhist monks and nuns are being urged to scrap a 1,000-year-old initiation rite of burning bare patches on the scalp because it is bad for their health.

Back of a lorry

Philadelphia, Feb 27.—An armoured van lost $1.2 in cash when its back door flew open and two bags containing the money fell out. Two men in a car pulled up, picked up the bags and drove off laughing.

Bus company to babysit for 12p

Lisbon, Dec 14.—Two " rolling nurseries " are being offered by Lisbon's public transport system to give parents a few carefree hours for Christmas shopping.

Children aged four to 10 will be entertained by cartoon films during an hour-and-a-half bus journey around the city at a cost of about 12p.

Gourmet dies in restaurant

Paris, Feb 6.—Henri Clos-Jouve, president of the Guild of French Gastronomic Journalists, died while ordering lunch in a Paris restaurant today. He was 80.

A food writer for 50 years, he was considered to be one of the leading French gourmets.

Bank robber asks for press coverage

Sao Paulo, May 16.—A man who said he needed money because he had just lost his job walked into the offices of O Estado de Sao Paulo and said he intended to rob a bank. He asked if the paper would be interested in covering the hold-up.

The newspaper said it regarded the man as " mentally unbalanced " but sent a reporter and a photographer to follow him anyway.

The man entered a bank and gave the manager a note saying he had two hand grenades. Twelve minutes later he walked out with £20,000 worth of Brazilian currency. Although the newspaper alerted police before the robbery the robber hailed a taxi and escaped.

Chinese plan to breed near-human monster

Peking, Dec 10

The Chinese authorities are considering the renewal of partly successful research on cross-breeding men with chimpanzees to found a strain of helots for economic and technical purposes.

The Shanghai newspaper, *Wen Aui Bao* said yesterday that a female chimpanzee became pregnant 13 years ago after being inseminated with a man's sperm.

Red Guards, however, smashed up the laboratory and the chimpanzee died, according to Mr Qi Yongxiang, identified only as a "researcher in medicine", in the north-eastern city of Shenyang.

Mr Qi's ambition is to create what he calls a "near-human ape". Through enlargement of its brain and tongue, it should be able to grasp simple concepts and talk some kind of language. Organs from the proposed monster would possibly prove useful as substitutes for human or artificial organs in transplant cases.

It could even drive a car, herd animals, protect forests and natural resources, and be used for exploration of the seabed, outer space and the centre of the Earth.

Asked whether the Earth was not already overpopulated with human beings, let alone hybrids, Mr Qi said that the aim would be to use them for the benefit of humanity.

Asked whether it was ethical to create such a hybrid, Mr Qi said that semen was of no account once it left the body, and could be disposed of like manure. The creature produced would be classed as an animal, so there need be no qualms about killing it when necessary.

Trouserless

Harare — A young Zimbabwean burglar was caught when he left his trousers at the scene of the crime. After removing his jeans, jacket and shoes to squeeze between antiburglar bars, on the window of a flat, he was surprised and fled, leaving his identity card in his pocket.

Costly first meal

The first meal for her husband being prepared after her marriage by Mrs Caroline Vaudrey, aged 23, of Moorland Road, Maghull, near Liverpool, ended in disaster last night when their new £17,500 semi-detached house and wedding gifts were wrecked when a cooker blew up.

Canal barge

Berlin, June 24.—The skipper and deckhand of the barge Deutschland, which collided with several bridges on a West Berlin canal today and left behind a fleet of dented ships, were given a blood-alcohol test by police. The vessel's licence was withdrawn.

Bowled out

Firemen had to use a saw and screwdriver to free Dawn Stanley, aged 15, of Arnold, Nottingham, when her thumb became stuck in one of the bowls at a Nottingham bowling alley.

Rude priest

Perth

A Roman Catholic priest, found guilty of indecent exposure while wearing a tiger-patterned G-string, was put on a six-month good behaviour bond yesterday.

Legs in shark

Miami — The dismembered legs of a man, apparently murdered, were found in the belly of a tiger shark caught by local fishermen off the Florida coast. Attempts were being made to match them with missing persons.

GIRLS IN PARK CAN CARRY ON GIGGLING

"Mild screams and girlish giggles" invading quiet summer nights near a park in Gillingham, Kent, have been pronounced another form of recreation and inoffensive by the town council's recreation committee.

For the past six months the council has left the gates of the park ulocked at night to save money on having to repair them. But residents cimplained about vandalism and courting couples, so the councillors had to decide whether the experiment had proved a success.

Their verdict was that courting couples could not be regarded as offensive and there was no need to lock the park at night. Councillors said the activities in question were only another form of recreation.

SEAT BELT TRAPS IRISH DRIVER

Traffic at Heathrow was halted yesterday morning by an Irish woman driver stuck in her seat belt with her skirt round her neck.

Miss Theresa Boynan was eventually freed by police who climbed into the back of her Volkswagen and released the belt with a screwdriver. Her efforts to wriggle herself out were foiled when her skirt became caught by the steering wheel.

Prisoner jammed in cell air vent

A man aged 25, who was on remand charged with robbery, tried to escape yesterday through an air vent in a cell at Paignton, Devon.

He got stuck with his left arm and head outside and shouted for help, waking a policeman who eventually had to remove bricks before the prisoner could be pushed back into his cell.

White elephant fit for a king

Bangkok, May 22.—A white elephant has been born in Thailand's southern Petchaburi province in what is considered a good omen for the reign of King Bhumibol.

The white elephant, the fourth to be found during the present reign, is to be examined by experts before being presented to the king.

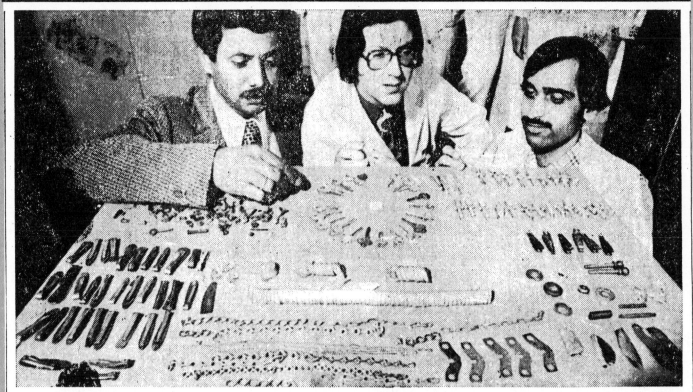

Hard tack: Doctors at the Metropolitan Hospital, New York, examining items removed from a mental patient's stomach. There were 300 coins and 200 other items, including broken thermometers, tin openers, eating utensils, keys, nuts, metal fragments and bolts. The man is recovering after a two-hour operation.

Jury sit for 27 seconds

The jury in the "handless corpse" murder and drug trial at Lancaster Crown Court were sent home until Monday because of legal arguments yesterday. They had been in court for 27 seconds.

Husband found wife with milkman

Sculptor jubilant at success of elephant safari

Nairobi, March 24

Mr Mihail Simeonov, a Bulgarian-born sculptor who lives in New York, is jubilant at the success of the first part of his plan to cast a limited edition of 10 life-size bronze statues of an African elephant.

A bull elephant was anaesthetized with a drugged dart on a ranch beneath Mount Kenya last week. It was then quickly coated with dental alginate.

Mr Simeonov plans to sell the 10 statues for $250,000 to benefit wild elephants.

Fugitives enlist aid of tigers to lose their pursuers

Hongkong, Oct 27

Hongkong's efforts to stem illegal immigration from China have revealed a curious new trade which has developed in the past six months: the sale of tiger's dung.

This, it seems, has become a successful dog repellent, the smell of which can be used to scare away bloodhounds used by Chinese Army units to track and pursue fugitives.

A group of young Chinese in Canton early this year decided to experiment with tiger-dung in their escape attempt and, it is reported, discovered that discreet scattering of the substance, sneaked from the city zoo, made the hounds keep a respectful distance.

The news was swiftly trans-

mitted to Canton after they reached Hongkong and a secret but brisk side-business was promoted by Triad gangs, who were organizing the mounting flood of illegal entrants into Hongkong.

Cantonese security authorities recently arrested some young men caught scraping the cages of tigers in the Canton zoo. Inquiries then uncovered the business which, it has been reported by local Kuomintang agents, had expanded into tiger-dung trafficking with rural residents of Hunan and Kwangsi provinces.

Prices reputedly ranged from the equivalent of £4 to £8 a basket. However, risky adulteration of pure tiger-dung has become common. "Pure for the rich illegals and adulterated for the poor", as the Kuomintang report claimed.

Pope rules out sex in afterlife

The Pope has affirmed that Catholic teaching excludes sexual activity in the afterlife, although the risen would still be male or female. He said the resurrection meant not only bodily recovery but a new state of life.

Robot kills man in factory

Tokyo.—A factory maintenance worker was fatally injured when a robot suddenly started up, struck him in the back and pinned him against another machine. It was Japan's first recorded death in a mishap involving an industrial robot.

The incident occurred last July at a Tokyo factory but was reported only after an investigation had been completed. The inquiry said the victim was guilty of carelessness but also found that safety measures in the plant were inadequate.

The clippings in this scrapbook have been taken from
The Times
The Sunday Times
The Observer
The Independent
The Guardian
The Daily Telegraph
The Sunday Telegraph
The Evening Standard
The Financial Times
The Sunday Correspondent

*Niki (Stefan Nekuda) is a cartoonist and professional
musician, living and working in Vienna, Austria. He can be
contacted through Collins & Brown.*

First published in Great Britain in 1990
by Collins & Brown Limited
Mercury House
195 Knightsbridge
London SW7 1RE

Copyright © Collins & Brown 1990

Illustrations copyright © Stefan Nekuda 1990

A CIP catalogue record for this book
is available from the British Library

ISBN 1 85585 006 0

Printed and bound in Great Britain
by Butler & Tanner, Frome